The Hi

BLACK COUNTRY

Aviation

The History of
BLACK COUNTRY
Aviation

A L E C   B R E W

ALAN SUTTON

First published in the United Kingdom in 1993 by
Alan Sutton Publishing Ltd · Phoenix Mill · Far Thrupp · Stroud · Gloucestershire

First published in the United States of America in 1993 by
Alan Sutton Publishing Inc. · 83 Washington Street · Dover · NH 03820

British Library Cataloguing in Publication Data

Brew, Alec
  History of Black Country Aviation:
  Balloons, Bleriots and Balliols
  I. Title
  629.1309424

ISBN 0-7509-0404-6

Library of Congress Cataloging in Publication Data applied for

Typeset in 10/12pt Times.
Typesetting and origination by
Alan Sutton Publishing Limited.
Printed in Great Britain by
Redwood Books, Trowbridge.

CONTENTS

Appendices

1

1862, WORLD ALTITUDE RECORD, WOLVERHAMPTON

If you were to try and choose the unlikeliest place from which to take off on a record breaking flight, Wolverhampton gasworks might spring to mind. If it did, you would be wrong, for in 1862 the world altitude record was broken in a flight that began at the gasworks on the Stafford Road. The gasworks was chosen because, of course, the craft involved was a balloon, and commercial coal gas was used rather than hydrogen to inflate it, being cheaper and far easier to obtain. Wolverhampton was chosen because it's about as far from the sea as you can get in this country, and the aviators involved had no wish to drift over the North Sea, or worse still the Atlantic.

The two men making the flight were a scientist, James Glaisher FRS, and a well-known balloonist named Henry Coxwell. Glaisher was Head of the Department of Magnetics and Meteorology at the Royal Observatory, Greenwich, and had long been convinced that balloons should be used for scientific investigation of the upper atmosphere.

Since the first flights of both hot-air and gas balloons in 1783, they had attracted little practical use. Scientific discoveries had been made – mostly of a negative nature in that formerly held theories were found to be so much eyewash – but no concerted attempt had been made to use balloons in a scientific manner.

Balloons had been used briefly for military observation purposes in the Napoleonic Wars. They had been very successful but had been discarded by the emperor himself. Possibly he felt they detracted from his own military prowess. They were to be used with similar brief success in the American Civil War, but the British Army had shown little interest in them.

In the main balloons were regarded as little more than a fairground attraction: professional airmen gave flights to wealthy patrons; huge crowds came to see balloons launched, latterly as much for the chance of seeing a terrible accident as the flight itself; successful balloonists travelled the country and used more and more tricks to attract paying spectators – acrobats were taken aloft, the first parachute drops were made, and even horses were lifted into the air slung beneath balloons.

As a surveyor in Ireland, Glaisher had developed an interest in meteorology from observing cloud formations from hilltops. He worked for a while at the observatory at Cambridge University, and was then appointed to his post at Greenwich in 1838.

It was from here, in 1852, that he watched a remarkable balloon flight by the celebrated airman, Charles Green, and John Welsh of Kew Observatory. Green's

James Glaisher, the meteorologist who conceived the idea of the high-altitude, scientific balloon flights from Wolverhampton, and became unconscious on the record-breaking ascent

balloon, the *Nassau*, was a giant of 70,000 cu. ft capacity, able to lift nearly 5,000 lb when inflated with hydrogen.

On their last of four flights together these two reached a height of nearly 23,000 ft. Because of exceptionally clear weather Glaisher was able to observe the whole of the flight through a telescope set up on the roof at Greenwich, and it was this which inspired him, in 1859, to persuade the British Association for the Advancement of Science to sponsor a research programme.

The purposes of the flights were to study the electrical, magnetic and oxygenic properties of the atmosphere at different altitudes, to compare different barometers and hygrometers, to examine the solar spectrum and solar radiation at higher altitudes and to study clouds and collect air from different elevations.

There were actually two reasons Glaisher proposed to make the flights from Wolverhampton. Apart from its distance from the sea, he also wanted to get away from the showground spectacle attitude to balloons in London.

Because of the difficulties in making and inflating balloons with hydrogen, it had become more usual to use commercial coal gas, which is why the Stafford Road gasworks was chosen for the launches. Coal gas could not lift as much as hydrogen, but its properties lended themselves to flights of longer duration. Mr Proud, manager of the Wolverhampton Gas Company was more than willing to co-operate. He not only

Henry Coxwell, one of the most
famous professional balloonists
of his day, who built and flew
the balloon

produced an unusually light gas, with a specific gravity between 320 and 350 as
opposed to the normal 530, but provided a special 60,000 cu. ft gas-holder to fill the
balloon.

The choice of a balloon was to prove a problem and was to delay the flights until
1862. Charles Green's *Nassau* was the obvious choice, but by now the balloon and its
famous pilot were both rather aged.

The *Nassau* was brought to Wolverhampton in August 1859, and Green was to fly it,
despite being seventy-four years of age. For the scientific observations, Glaisher
planned to send two young observers, rather than to go up himself. Unfortunately the
23-year-old balloon was so badly torn by the wind during both the attempted inflations
that its use had to be abandoned.

In 1861 a Balloon Committee of the British Association was formed in Oxford. As
well as its chairman, Colonel Sykes, it included Glaisher, Sir David Brewster, Sir John
Herschel and Lord Wrottesley. They voted funds for a series of scientific balloon
flights to commence in 1862.

The chosen balloon was the 30-year old *Royal Normandy* of H. Lithgoe, which was
rather smaller than the *Nassau*. Lithgoe arrived in Wolverhampton with his balloon on
21 March 1862, and inflation commenced on the following day. Mr H.C. Chiswick was
to ascend with Lithgoe to make the scientific observations.

The ascent commenced at 1.40 p.m., but the old balloon was leaking from the very start. It rose to a height of one mile, but they had to throw out almost all the ballast. They descended towards Chillington Pool, and desperately threw out the last bag of ballast to avoid landing in the water. They landed in a field on one of the Chillington Farms, and had an inhospitable reception. Once the locals had discovered that the pilots were unhurt, they left them, and Lithgoe and Chiswick had a devil of a job finding a vehicle to take them back to Wolverhampton. This shows just how blasé even country folk had become over balloons.

Lithgoe went straight off to London by train and returned with Henry Coxwell and his smaller balloon, *Mars*. Unfortunately this had recently been damaged in a flight at Newport, Monmouth, and could not be repaired in time for use by the British Association, so Coxwell offered to make a giant balloon for use later in the year, and the Balloon Committee accepted.

It was made of American cloth rather than the more usual silk, and had a capacity of 90,000 cu. ft. Coxwell later christened it *The Mammoth*. Glaisher changed his mind about flying himself, and the flights were now re-scheduled for late 1862.

The early flights

The first ascent was made on 17 July. They took off from the Stafford Road works at 9.43 a.m. to the cheers of the spectators (including Lord Wrottesley), few in number, as the flight had been kept largely secret. The orange balloon was in sight of the crowd for only ten minutes before disappearing into the clouds. They reached a height of 26,000 ft. Coxwell concentrated on flying the balloon, while Glaisher made a series of observations with his instruments; but they took time to toast the Queen, the British Association, Lord Wrottesley and the town and people of Wolverhampton, with wine they had thoughtfully included in their supplies.

After some time Coxwell feared that they might be blown out over the Wash, and they descended quickly, picking up a great deal of water vapour as they passed through thick cloud. This resulted in a rather heavy landing in Langham, Rutland, near the house of Mr E. Baker, breaking many of Glaisher's instruments. Mr Baker, being rather more hospitable than the Chillington farmworkers, gave the pilots dinner and then conveyed them to the station, with the balloon, and they arrived back in Wolverhampton that evening.

The balloon was then taken down to Crystal Palace, where it made three flights of much lower altitude, 16,790 ft, 7,380 ft and 6,890 ft respectively. Glaisher was able to make observations at a lower altitude, which had proved impossible at Wolverhampton owing to the rapid rate of ascent.

The second flight from Wolverhampton was made on 18 August, taking off at 1.02 p.m. in clear weather. Lord and Lady Wrottesley were present with about three hundred other spectators. The take-off was delayed while Mr Carl Holt photographed the balloon. They reached a height of 23,700 ft and as they finally descended, were treated to the sight of the balloon's shadow on the Earth surrounded by prismatic

The Mammoth making its second ascent from the Stafford Road gasworks, Wolverhampton. The railway viaduct in the background is still there (Wolverhampton Central Library)

colours. At 4.25 p.m. the balloon made a gentle landing in Solihull. The changing altitudes and lack of oxygen at height gave Glaisher an intense headache that lasted for hours afterwards.

Higher than Everest

The third and last flight from Wolverhampton began just after 1 p.m. on Friday, 5 September. The late start had been caused by bad weather in the morning, and it was still only 59°F and heavily overcast when they finally took off. They were watched once more by Lord and Lady Wrottesley, and various directors of the gas company, as well as the Mayor of Wolverhampton.

At 11,000 ft they broke out of the cloud into beautiful sunshine. At three miles altitude they threw out the first of the pigeons they had taken, but the poor beast fell to earth like a lump of lead. In 1 hour and 40 minutes after take-off they were four miles high and rising rapidly. They threw out the second and third pigeon, which fell after their compatriot vainly attempting to fly. The fourth pigeon must have been made of sterner stuff, managing to alight on top of the balloon for a while, though they never saw it again.

Glaisher lies unconscious in the basket as Coxwell ascends to free the valve line; they were probably higher than the summit of Mount Everest

Within ten minutes they had climbed another mile. Coxwell concentrated on flying the balloon and discharging more ballast-sand, while Glaisher continued to make scientific observations. Because of his physical exertions in throwing out some 2,000 lb of ballast, Coxwell had begun to have difficulty breathing before Glaisher, but after 1 hour 52 minutes of the flight they both began experiencing the effects of oxygen deprivation. Glaisher could no longer see the hands of his watch, or the column of mercury in the thermometer, and asked Coxwell to read the instruments for him.

Owing to the imbalance in the basket, the balloon had revolved since its take-off, and the valve line had become entangled. Coxwell now had to climb out of the basket and up into the ring which held the lines above their heads. Glaisher estimated their height to be 29,000 ft at that moment.

Glaisher found he could not move his arms, and then when he attempted to move his head it flopped sideways onto his shoulder. He collapsed backwards, his head resting on the side of the basket from where he could watch Coxwell in the rigging above him, struggling with the valve line. His vision clouded over and eventually he became unconscious.

Coxwell experienced severe cold, and there was hoar frost all round the ring. The self-recording thermometer was to record −20F, or 52° of frost. His hands were so frozen he could not grip anything, and to return to the basket he had to rest his arms on the ring and drop down into it. He felt his senses leaving him and was desperate to pull the valve line to release gas and stop their ascent. Because his hands were immobile he took the line in his teeth and pulled it two or three times as hard as he could, and to his relief the balloon began to descent rapidly. If he had lost consciousness like Glaisher they would have almost certainly died, and the balloon would eventually have expanded so much it might well have burst.

Coxwell attempted to rouse Glaisher, who gradually regained consciousness. 'I have been insensible', he said, and Coxwell replied, 'You have, and I too, very nearly.' At 2 hours and 7 minutes since take-off Glaisher was able to resume his observations.

The height they had actually reached could only be an estimate. When Glaisher became unconscious they had been ascending at 1,000 ft a minute, and when he regained his senses after 7 minutes they were descending at twice that rate. He estimated that they had reached an altitude of 37,000 ft, seven miles above the earth.

The rapid descent continued and Coxwell landed the balloon safely in a large meadow belonging to a Mr Kexallat at Cold Weston, near the village of Clee St Margaret on the western side of the Brown Clee Hill. As they neared the ground numerous locals ran after them, but on landing the locals were too frightened to

Captain Morton's balloon, *Dudley Castle*, ascending from the Molineux Gardens on 11 September 1882, with Colonel Thorneycroft of Tettenhall as a passenger. They landed at Smethwick an hour later, flying little higher than the rooftops for most of the way (Wolverhampton Central Library)

approach the balloon and huddled in a group in the corner of the field. Clearly the ordinary folk out in the depths of Shropshire were rather less worldly wise than those nearer to the Black Country.

One of the remaining two pigeons, which they had not released, had died, the other eventually revived and they released it, but it was never seen again. Despite his arduous experience and being fifty-three years old, Glaisher then had to walk over seven miles into Ludlow to fetch a horse and cart to retrieve the balloon from where Coxwell remained on guard.

Both Glaisher and Coxwell were to make many more balloon flights and reached ripe old ages, a not too common achievement of balloonists of the time. Glaisher became a founder member of The Royal Aeronautical Society, and was to become its chairman.

Glaisher's estimate of 37,000 ft has since been challenged, but there is no doubt that they achieved well in excess of 30,000 ft, higher than Mount Everest. It was a heroic feat by any standards, and a record not approached until 1901, when a German balloon

Another balloon ascent from the Molineux Gardens, on 25 May 1901, by a balloon advertising Hudson's Soap. At this time the Molineux had become the Wolves' football ground (Wolverhampton Central Library)

filled with hydrogen and with oxygen equipment for the crew, achieved 35,500 ft. This record was only broken by balloons using pressurized gondolas.

Glaisher and Coxwell almost certainly reached a height no one has ever attained without the use of oxygen. They came perilously close to dying, and there is also little doubt that this record will stand for all time.

2
1902, Man-Lifting Kites, Wolverhampton

In 1902 the first recorded flights by a man in a heavier-than-air craft in the Black Country took place in Wolverhampton. The craft involved was a most unusual one, a man-lifting kite built by the showman S.F. Cody.

Samuel Franklin Cody, no relation whatsoever to the contemporary Buffalo Bill Cody, was a Texan who came to Europe in the nineteenth century with a sharp-shooting act. He married an Englishwoman and settled in Britain, performing in numerous venues. He had developed an interest in kites when, as a boy back in Texas, a Chinese cook taught him their principles on cattle drives.

The Wild West Showman, Samuel Cody, at the controls of one of his huge biplanes, popularly called *Cathedrals* (R.T. Edwards)

In 1901, when touring Britain in a western play he had written himself, entitled *Klondyke Nugget*, he developed the idea of building a man-lifting kite. He had considered the difficulties the British Army was having during the Boer War in operating observation balloons in high winds, and thought that a kite was the obvious answer, because kites thrive in high winds.

Building a man-lifting kite had been tried before, without much success, notably by Captain B.F.S. Baden-Powell, brother of the founder of the scouting movement. Cody chose the box-kite developed by the Australian, Laurence Hargreave, as the basis for his man-lifter. He planned to fly a train of them, but on a single cable, unlike the two-cable scheme used by Baden-Powell.

The kite's development was a piecemeal, trial and error, process. Cody was hampered by the fact that he was touring the country with *Klondyke Nugget* and could only work on his kite in odd moments. Drawing on the memories of bird-shaped kites he had built in his childhood, he eventually tried out a box-kite with triangular extensions in the form of wing tips. This produced a kite that was admirably stable.

He slowly developed a procedure for flying a train of such kites. He would send up a small pilot kite attached to up to 1,000 ft of piano wire. To this was attached a cable, eventually an inch in diameter with a breaking strain of two tons. When the pilot kite

A soldier ascending in one of Cody's War Kites. The cable is held aloft by a number of lifter kites. It was this system with which Cody was experimenting when he came to Wolverhampton in 1902 with his Wild West Show *Klondyke Nugget* (R.T. Edwards)

had lifted several hundred feet of this cable, the lifter kites, attached to fairleads, were sent up it one by one until they were halted by stop-cleats gripping on steel balls. As many as ten of these would be sent aloft, depending on the strength of the wind, and the height required.

As each kite went up more and more cable was paid out from the winch. The purpose of the lifters was purely to hold up the cable. The man, sitting in a little wicker basket, was carried aloft beneath another kite, 19 ft in diameter. He controlled his ascent by a brake consisting of a copper-jawed trolley that clamped on the cable.

To descend he pulled on a bridle, which altered the angle of the carrier kite to reduce lift, let go the brake, and the kite slid down the cable at a slow steady rate. Cody himself made the first flight, and in 1901 he patented his device and offered it to the War Office. They turned him down, but he continued to develop his invention, adding such refinements as a telephone for an observer to make his reports to the ground.

He was still touring the country in *Klondyke Nugget*, and flew his kites in many cities, usually causing the police a great deal of trouble as huge crowds gathered to watch. When *Klondyke Nugget* came to Wolverhampton in 1902, he flew his kite from the West Park, but the police asked him to stop because the crowds were trampling the flower beds!

Cody was eventually to convince the War Office of the viability of his invention, and they adopted his War Kite, as he called it. He was to move on to greater things. He built the first powered aircraft to fly in Britain, achieved in October 1908; in 1909 he became a British citizen and in 1912 his Cody Flyer V won the first military trials to be held in Britain. Sadly, in August 1913 a seaplane he had built broke up in the air and he was killed. Over 100,000 people lined the route for his funeral, acknowledging him as a national hero.

Cody was one of the greatest pioneers of flight in this country, and Wolverhampton just missed a second chance of seeing him in action. In 1910 the first aerial meeting of the year was held at Dunstall Park, but Cody could not attend because of damage done in tests to his Cody Flyer II.

3

1905, BY AIRSHIP FROM AMBELCOTE TO BRIERLEY HILL

During the nineteenth century balloon flights were commonplace throughout the Black Country. The celebrated balloonist G.P. Lampriere made thirty-nine ascents from Dudley Castle alone, and also made the first ascent at Wolverhampton Flower Show. The Corbett Hospital Fête at Ambelcote also had a balloon ascent each year, but in 1905 the committee decided to invite Stanley Spencer to demonstrate his airship.

Stanley Spencer was the son of Charles Green Spencer, who had been named after Charles Green, the celebrated Victorian balloonist. C.G. Spencer's father was Edward Spencer who had been a great friend of Charles Green, and made many flights with him in his balloon, the *Nassau*, the first balloon James Glaisher had brought to Wolverhampton.

Charles Spencer founded a company in Highbury, Messrs. C.G. Spencer & Sons, manufacturing balloons and parachutes. His son, Stanley Spencer, became a professional aeronaut, building and flying balloons professionally. For instance, in 1901 he took the Hon. C.S. Rolls for a flight in one of his balloons, and Rolls was so enthralled by the experience he went on to become an eminent balloonist himself.

On 22 September 1902 Spencer had become the first Englishman to build and fly a successful airship. His first was 75 ft long with a diameter of 20 ft, and a capacity of 20,000 cu. ft. It was powered by a water-cooled $3\frac{1}{2}$ h.p. Simms engine which ran at a remarkable 2500 r.p.m., geared down to drive a 10 ft wooden propeller at 250 r.p.m. Beneath the envelope there was a 42 ft bamboo girder from which hung the 4 ft long, one-man car, and the engine.

On 22 September Spencer flew this first airship from Crystal Palace over Battersea, Earls Court and Acton, before landing after a rather erratic flight at Eastcote. The success of this one hour flight encouraged him to build a much larger airship, but on at least one occasion the envelope folded up when it was inflated.

The airship Stanley Spencer brought to Stourbridge was of 40,000 cu. ft. It was 84 ft long and 30 ft in diameter, powered by a $4\frac{1}{2}$ h.p. Simms engine driving a tractor propeller at 150 r.p.m. In still air it was capable of driving the airship at 10–15 m.p.h.

The gondola was of triangular construction made of bamboo with wire bracing, suspended from a sailcloth cover over the envelope, which Spencer hoped would act as a parachute if there was a sudden deflation. There were automatic valves to release gas if too much pressure built up on the ascent. The craft was steered by two ropes which altered the angle of the propeller.

Stanley Spencer's airship en route from Ambelcote's Corbett Hospital Fête to Brierley Hill in August 1905 (R.T. Edwards)

Spencer had already made seven flights in the airship, at London, Shrewsbury, Hanley, and York, before coming to Stourbridge; as well as thirty-one in his other airships. He believed in self-advertisement, and usually only flew when sponsored. His longest had been 32 miles starting at Crystal Palace.

The airship was inflated at Stourbridge gasworks on Monday, 7 August 1905, the first day of the fête. He used coal gas because it only cost £7–£8 to fill the envelope, whereas hydrogen would cost around £150, though it had twice the lifting capacity.

At around 6.30 p.m. everything was finally ready and Spencer took off to enthusiastic applause. He turned and flew with the light breeze towards Brierley Hill. He manoeuvred and turned again, but an impending storm forced him to land on the golf course at Scotts Green, from where it was brought back to Ambelcote on a cart.

The following day Spencer avoided probing questions about the ability of the airship to fly against the wind. Clearly the low power of the engine and the size of the envelope, caused from his use of coal gas, made it almost impossible for him to make progress against anything but the lightest of breezes. As if to prove the point he then made an almost identical flight, travelling with the breeze, and landing at Brierley Hill.

These two short flights were the first by a powered flying machine within the Black Country. It was to be another five years before a heavier-than-air machine made a successful powered flight in the area, but a Dudley man was shortly to embark on a career which would make him the leading pre-war aircraft designer in this country.

4

1907, THE WRIGHT BROTHERS FROM DUDLEY

It is a little known fact that the aviation pioneers, the Wright Brothers, came from Dudley. Not Orville and Wilbur, of course, but Howard and Warwick Wright, who, for a short while were considered to be the foremost aircraft constructors in Great Britain, rivalling the Short Brothers' claim to have been the first aircraft manufacturers in this country.

They and their brother Walter were the sons of Joseph Wright who owned a chainmaking company in Tipton, which also made boilers and pithead gear. Howard served an engineering apprenticeship in the firm, which was sold in 1889 to the

Howard Theophilus Wright, born in Dudley, the greatest unsung aircraft pioneer in this country, pictured in 1912 (R.C. Hunt)

prominent industrialist Hiram Maxim. Maxim was in the process of developing a lightweight steam engine to power a huge biplane he was building.

It seems that Howard became involved in this project and was to register a number of patents for steam boilers. In 1894 Maxim's aircraft made a 'flight' of 600 ft from a track which was designed to prevent it rising more than a couple of feet above the ground. It tore free from the track and was severely damaged. Maxim abandoned it and began a long series of experiments with a view to building another aircraft. Some of these experiments involved testing aerofoil sections at the end of a revolving arm.

In 1905 the three brothers formed their own company, Howard T. Wright Bros. Ltd to develop Howard's inventions and to deal in motor cars. In 1906 Warwick Wright Ltd was also formed to build and sell cars. Howard Wright's interest in aviation was undiminished, and when he met a like-minded enthusiast, William Oke Manning, they decided to go into the business of constructing flying machines.

A helicopter ordered

An Italian inventor, Federico Capone, had built an unsuccessful helicopter and approached Hiram Maxim for advice. He was referred to Howard Wright, and an

Warwick Wright, co-constructor with his brother Howard of some of the earliest successful aircraft in this country, pictured between the wars at the Short Bros. factory at Rocester. In 1909 the Short Bros. and the Wright Bros. had neighbouring workshops under Battersea railway arches (R.C. Hunt)

agreement was reached for Warwick Wright Ltd to design and construct a new helicopter to Capone's general outline. In 1907 construction started in the motor works, but a new factory was quickly established in a railway arch at Battersea, where one of their neighbours were the Short Brothers, who were at the time the official balloon-makers for the Royal Aero Club.

At the time there was a handful of pioneers in this country attempting, so far unsuccessfully, to build their own flying machines: S.F. Cody, John William Dunne, A.V. Roe and Horatio Phillips. The Short Brothers did not receive their first order for a heavier-than-air machine until shortly afterwards, when Moore-Brabazon ordered a glider, so the Wright Brothers could correctly claim to be the first aircraft factory in this country, and the Capone helicopter was the first of about forty aircraft that they were to build.

The helicopter had a framework of steel tube, made by Accles & Pollock of Oldbury, and two 26 ft rotors, each with two blades. It was powered by a 30 h.p. Antoinette engine, which also drove two small four-blade propellers for forward thrust. There were also vertical and horizontal surfaces to relieve the load on the rotors.

In 1908 it achieved a tethered flight on Norbury Golf Course and lifted a total weight of 650 lb. Signor Capone took it to Italy, but further tests in Naples were unsuccessful. Undaunted Signor Capone returned to England and had Wright design him another helicopter. Obviously feeling he needed to hedge his bets, he also had Wright design and build an ornithopter.

Howard Wright's helicopter was the first in Britain to leave the ground, though there was little or no means of controlling it. The first helicopter in the world to leave the ground was the Breguet Gyroplane No. 1, which left the ground on 29 September 1907, but needed four men to hold it steady. Two weeks later another French design by Paul Curnu was the first to leave the ground in free flight.

Wright's ornithopter can have had little more success than was usual with such contraptions, in any case Signor Capone abandoned both systems. Howard Wright's achievement in building three aircraft for one customer was something his contemporaries would not attain for some time.

Moore-Brabazon's Shorts'-built glider was housed in a shed at Brooklands racing track, alongside another where a young man, Alliott Verdon Roe, was trying in vain to get a tractor-biplane with a tiny 9 h.p. JAP engine into the air. In 1908 Howard Wright was commissioned to re-design the glider to take a 12 h.p. Buchet engine, and he also changed the elevator and rudder design. Moore-Brabazon never tried out his aircraft, except as a kite. Instead he went to France and bought a Voisin Biplane, with which he made the first flight by a British subject on 1 December 1908.

The 1908 biplane

In 1908, still in the Battersea railway arches, Howard Wright, helped by William Manning, built a biplane of their own design for Malcolm Seton-Karr, and this was shown at the Aero Show at Olympia in 1908. Of eleven complete aircraft at the show, there were only three that were British. The other two were the frame of the Short No. 1, Wright-type biplane, and a small monoplane on Frederick Handley Page's stand, but built by the Weiss Aeroplane and Launcher Syndicate Ltd. It could be said that Howard Wright's aircraft was the only practical aircraft in existence designed by an Englishman.

Howard Wright's machine had several very advanced design features, which indicated Howard Wright's background in engineering. There was an enclosed nacelle for the pilot, and extensive use was made of welded steel tubing in its construction. The 50 h.p. water-cooled Metallurgique engine drove contra-rotating, co-axial propellers. It had a single main wheel and further wheels at the tips of the wings.

The span was 40 ft and the length 43 ft, with an empty weight of 1,600 lb. The aircraft was tested later at Fambridge in Essex and several straight hops were achieved. The undercarriage arrangement proved a problem as the machine leaned on one or other of the wing-tip wheels, and a speed approaching 20 m.p.h. had to be attained before it became level. Also Seton-Karr had to teach himself to fly as well as test the aircraft at the same time. There was trouble with the contra-rotating propellers before delivery of the machine to Rye Harbour in Sussex.

The monoplanes

Having built a helicopter, an ornithopter and a pusher biplane, Howard Wright showed his versatility, or perhaps his uncertainty, by building, later in 1909, a tractor monoplane. It was powered by a 35 h.p., four-cylinder Lascelles engine, and had an empty weight of 480 lb. Its span was 28 ft and its length 27 ft. The fact that Wright now believed himself to be on the right lines was shown by the fact that his next design was a very similar machine, his Avis monoplane.

The Avis was designed for the Scottish Aeroplane Syndicate and had the same dimensions as his earlier monoplane, though it weighed 50 lb less. The prototype was powered by a three-cylinder 30 h.p. Anzani engine, and flew early in 1910 at Brooklands. Wright had abandoned his metal-tube construction and built a wire-braced wooden girder fuselage of what was at the time very conventional design. It had wing-warping like the earlier monoplane, and two pairs of rubber-sprung main wheels.

It was exhibited at that year's Olympia Aero Show, and advertised at £370, not including engine. The prototype was sold to the Hon. Alan R. Boyle, and he used it to gain his Aviator's Certificate No. 13 at Brooklands on 14 June 1910. The Avis was one of the first successful British monoplanes and three more were built, powered by 40 h.p. eight-cylinder JAP engines.

The Wrights built another monoplane during 1909, this time a two-seater powered by a 50 h.p. Antoinette steam-cooled engine which drove two co-axial propellers, though these were later replaced by a single propeller. The condensers for the steam-cooling were sited as long panels on the fuselage sides. There was a large gap between the passenger, who was seated centrally to the wings, and the pilot, who sat well back in the fuselage.

Alan Boyle on his Howard Wright Avis monoplane at Dunstall Park, Wolverhampton, 1910. The Avis was the first successful British monoplane, and the first type that T.O.M. Sopwith owned (Jim Boulton)

In 1909 the Wrights also built two monoplanes designed by Horatio Barber for the Aeronautical Syndicate Ltd, a company Barber set up in another of the Battersea railway arches. The aircraft were an unsuccessful tractor monoplane, and a pusher that managed to fly, and which formed the basis for a series of aircraft that Barber subsequently built in new facilities at Hendon.

Teaching Tommy Sopwith to fly

After a revised version of the Avis powered by a 40 h.p. ENV engine, and with an altered tail, Howard Wright's next design was the aircraft for which he is most well known, his 1910 biplane. It was a conventional two-seat pusher with a 60 h.p. ENV engine, a forward elevator on Farman lines, and ailerons on all four wings. It was shown at the 1911 Olympia Aero Show.

It has achieved fame because it is the aircraft on which T.O.M. Sopwith learned to fly. On 22 October 1910, having just bought an Avis monoplane, Sopwith took off at Brooklands, never having flown before, and not surprisingly crashed. He was unhurt

T.O.M. Sopwith and his sister on his Howard Wright biplane, the aircraft in which he learned to fly (R.C. Hunt)

and a month later, this time in a brand-new Howard Wright biplane, he taught himself to fly and gained his Aviator's Certificate No. 31 all in only a day.

Only three weeks later he entered the Baron de Forest contest for the longest all-British flight into Europe, and achieved a flight of 169 miles from Eastchurch, on the Isle of Sheppey, to Thirimont, Belgium. Sopwith later took his Howard Wright on a tour of America. Eleven of the biplanes were built and in 1912 one of them was flown as far away as Rangoon, Burma, by W. England. Yet another became the first aircraft to fly successfully in New Zealand.

The business is sold

During 1911 Warwick Wright Ltd, including the services of the two brothers and W.O. Manning, was bought out by the Coventry Ordnance Works, and Howard began designing two aircraft for the 1912 Military Trials.

They were both broadly similar two-seat tractor biplanes with enclosed fuselages, one with 100 h.p. Gnome engine had side-by-side seating and the other, with a 110 h.p.

Chenu engine, had tandem seating. Though the metal parts were built in Coventry, the aircraft were assembled in the Battersea workshop.

T.O.M. Sopwith was engaged as the pilot but neither of the biplanes was very successful, there were problems with the engines and propellers. Howard Wright left the company and became the manager of the newly-formed aviation department of J. Samuel White & Co., of East Cowes, Isle of Wight, a constructor of destroyers and marine diesel engines.

He began building a seaplane with a wing section with two points of maximum camber, which he hoped would be a great improvement on the conventional wing section, giving a wide speed range. Unfortunately such a design gave inherently high drag, though it was not immediately clear, as the biplane structure with multi-strutted floats had a high degree of drag in any case, largely compensated by the fact that a large two-row Gnome radial of 160 h.p. was fitted.

The Wight No. 1 double-camber navyplane first flew in 1913, and Wright embarked on an improved version, the Wight No. 2 navyplane, which was exhibited at the 1913 Olympia Aero Show. It was intended as a reconnaissance and training aircraft, and was also tested as a landplane.

The concept was further advanced with a larger seaplane built in 1914, and powered by a 200 h.p. Canton Unne radial. It was much larger than the No. 2 navyplane, with a span of 63 ft and an empty weight of 3,500 lb. It first flew on 7 April, and a number were ordered and delivered to the Royal Navy by the end of May. One example was sold to Germany.

Later in 1914 J. Samuel White & Co. received an order for an Admiralty design, the A.D. 1000. This was a very large seaplane with a 115 ft span, designed to be powered by two 310 h.p. Sunbeam engines. Howard Wright extensively redesigned it, improving it greatly. Trouble with the Sunbeam engines caused some delay and it was eventually fitted with 200 h.p. Canton Unne engines.

During the First World War Wright was to design a large number of aircraft for the White Company, all of them with his double-camber aerofoil sections. Their overall success was perhaps held back because of the dichotomy of interest, with Samuel White's naval production taking precedence.

It is hard to understand why Howard Wright is not more well known; why the Wright Brothers from Dudley are not acclaimed as the important pioneers that they were. In 1907 and 1908 Howard Wright was clearly ahead of both Dunne and Roe in the development of a practical aircraft and well ahead of them in the understanding of aerodynamics. He was also at least on a par with Cody, who was still an American citizen. Wright was therefore indisputably the leading British pioneer of the time, perhaps unsurprisingly given his excellent engineering background and the work he had done with Maxim.

He seems to have been a diffident character, lacking the driving force which carried Roe and Cody, and others such as Frederick Handley Page and Geoffrey de Havilland, ever forward in their determination to perfect and produce their own designs. From the outset he seems to have been happy to work for other people, even to build other

people's designs. The others were to do this as well, but only for the financial rewards which would help them with their own projects. Even when he had produced Britain's first successful monoplane, the Avis, and then the highly successful biplane, he seems to have been happy to allow the Coventry Ordnance Works to take over his company, and later on to go on to merely work for Samuel White & Co.

His aircraft were of advanced construction, his 1908 biplane had a sturdy metal frame, when Roe was building the flimsiest wooden structures imaginable. Only the Short brothers, of the early pioneers, equalled his workmanship, and his 1910 biplane was still setting high standards of construction. Although he was happy for people to commission designs from him based on their own ideas, he was innovatory, and even revolutionary. The nacelle on his 1908 biplane, and the contra-rotating propellers were far ahead of their time.

Howard Wright should be hailed alongside Cody and Roe, and the fact that he is not, is surprising. Dudley has a son to be proud, if only it knew it.

5

1910, DUNSTALL PARK AVIATION MEETING, WOLVERHAMPTON

The year 1909 was a momentous one for British aviation. The Channel flight of Louis Bleriot on 25 July, and the news of the achievements of the French pioneers, especially at the aviation meeting at Rheims, completely changed the attitude of the British public. The country went aviation crazy.

The handful of British pioneers, who in 1908 received little but derision in the way of recognition, were now joined by many more. Cody on 16 October 1908 had made the first recognized flight in Britain, though he was still an American citizen. Alliott Verdon Roe was still trying to build an aircraft on a shoestring, and making his first small hops at Brooklands, before being ejected as an embarrassment by the track management.

In late 1908 Lancelot Gibbs had tested Dunne's first powered aircraft, the swept-winged, tailless D.4 with two Buchet engines supposedly giving 30 h.p., but actually giving more like 12 h.p. It failed to leave the ground, but in December, refitted with a 30 h.p. Antoinette, it managed a few bounds of 40 yards.

Throughout 1909 the French still led the way, and it was to France that wealthy prospective aviators largely turned to buy their machines, Farman and Voisin biplanes, and Antoinette and Bleriot monoplanes.

Warwick Wright Ltd and the Short Bros. were the first British aircraft factories. Others were to follow, among them the Humber Car Company of Coventry, who were to build complete Bleriot monoplanes including propellers and engines. Many individuals were also to attempt to build and fly their own aircraft. In June 1909 there were at least thirty such people in Britain, some of them subsequently famous such as Geoffrey de Havilland, Frederick Handley Page and Harold Blackburn, and numerous others who were to become only footnotes in aviation history.

There were two flying meetings in Britain in 1909 – at Doncaster, where Cody became a British citizen, and Blackpool; but the first of 1910 and only the third in all was to be at Wolverhampton.

The Midland Aero Club

On 3 September 1909 a crowded meeting called by Mr W. Ivy-Rogers had unanimously agreed to form a Midland Aero Club. Mr Ivy-Rogers had obviously been bitten by the aviation bug after he had been taken up for a flight by S.F. Cody, which lasted all of 4 minutes. He was elected the club's first Honorary Secretary. There were a hundred people willing to pay the subscription of one guinea, or half a guinea for minors.

To begin with, model flying was undertaken in Sutton Park, and on 13 November a full-size glider was present, flown by J.H. Else, or rather not flown, as after several runs down the hill it failed to become airborne. In March 1910, at the invitation of the racecourse company, the club adopted Dunstall Park, Wolverhampton, as its first headquarters and then they arranged what was billed as the first All-British Flying Meeting, to begin on 27 June.

The newspapers of the day had helped spur aviation by offering large cash prizes for various flights, such as the *Daily Mail*'s offer of £10,000 for the first flight from London to Manchester. Flying meetings, such as that at Dunstall Park, also offered cash prizes for various flying competitions as well as appearance money. The Midland Aero Club offered £1,000 for the pilot who made the flights of the longest total duration at the meeting, a trophy for the pilot who made the fastest three circuits of the course, and £300 for the longest cross-country flight round a course that went via Albrighton, Cosford Water Works and Tettenhall.

There were also smaller prizes such as £100 for the shortest 'get-off' (take-off run), and £100 for the best 'figure flying', together with special prizes for the best flights by members of the club itself.

These cash prizes were the only way that professional aviators, such as Cody and Roe, and enthusiastic amateurs such as Charles Rolls, and Cecil Grace, could finance their flying; and it was a way of attracting the best-known names of the day, in order to draw big crowds to defray the costs. These 'star' names changed almost day by day as new records were broken all the time.

Although the Meeting did not start until 27 June, by the 6th there were already three aircraft in residence in the six wooden hangars, which had been erected by the Midlands Aviation Syndicate, the company set up to run the meeting. They were in a row by the Birmingham Canal, next to the railway viaduct.

Only pilots who had obtained one of the new Aviator's Certificates, of which only sixteen had so far been granted, would be eligible to fly in the Meeting. Anyone else had to bring their aircraft along early, and obtain their Certificate before the Meeting started.

Arriving early was a Bleriot monoplane owned by a serving army officer, Captain George William Patrick Dawes, a Humber monoplane owned by Mr N. Holder of Edgbaston, the son of Sir John Holder (who offered a trophy at the Meeting for the highest flight), and a Star monoplane.

The Star monoplane

The Star had been built by Star Engineering of Frederick Street, Wolverhampton, one of the premier motor car manufacturers in the country. Like many others, its proprietor, Edward Lisle, had been inspired to indulge in the new 'sunrise industry' of aeroplane

The Star monoplane at the Olympia Aero Show of 1910, in the form in which it competed unsuccessfully at Dunstall Park (Jim Boulton)

construction. To design the aircraft and its engine he had engaged the services of an outgoing, energetic young man, Granville Eastwood Bradshaw, who would also undertake the role of his own test pilot, while learning to fly at the same time. That was the way all the pioneers did it.

Granville Bradshaw, who was born in Preston in 1892, had formed an engine company earlier in 1910. He called it the All-British Engine Company, later to become just ABC. The engine in the Star was his first design and was built by Star Engineering. It was a four-cylinder water-cooled in-line which gave 40 h.p. at 1,450 r.p.m. It weighed 175 lb including the water pump and Simms magneto, and had a bore of 4 in and a stroke of 5 in.

The Star monoplane was built on the lines of the French Antoinette, but had a rather unusual tailplane which incorporated all the control surfaces within its four planes like those of a dart, each twisting in an opposite direction to the other. The engine drove a 6 ft 8 in propeller. The aircraft had been exhibited at the Olympia Aero Show, back in April, where it was offered for sale at £450.

The Hartill monoplane

Another Wolverhampton-built monoplane appeared shortly after the Star. It had been designed by Edgar Hartill, a plumbing contractor of Cleveland Street, Wolverhampton, to the order of a Dr Hands. It was built on the lines of Santos Dumont's Demoiselle,

The Wolverhampton-built Hartill monoplane at Dunstall Park. Edgar Hartill is seated at the controls, and Dr Hands, for whom the aircraft was built, is standing at the wing-tip (Fred Mason, via Jim Boulton)

and had been exhibited in a shop in Darlington Street for a while. It was powered by an Alvaston 20 h.p. engine.

Another member of the Midland Aero Club, Lt. John Seddon of the Royal Navy, entered a tandem-winged biplane for which he had to build a larger seventh hangar, but his aircraft was not completed in time to take part.

Early flights

By 8 June the crowds gathering at Dunstall Park were already numbered in the hundreds, and they were rewarded by the first tentative flights. Captain Dawes took his Bleriot up to 20–25 ft but did not yet attempt a turn, and Bradshaw managed a few brief hops in the Star.

On 9 June Dawes was in the air again, but Bradshaw announced that he was waiting for a 'stronger propeller' for the Star. Meanwhile the Hartill monoplane was being erected in one of the hangars. On 10 June Mr Holder made his first short flights in the Humber, reaching a height of 15–20 ft on two occasions. The crowd gave him a burst of applause for his efforts.

The following morning Captain Dawes made the most ambitious flight to date. He managed to circle the racecourse twice; repeating the feat after breakfast. At the time

A Bleriot or Humber monoplane flying over Dunstall Park, possibly that of Captain Dawes (Ken Robinson via Jim Boulton)

the principles of turning an aircraft were not fully understood. Rather than banking the aircraft with a co-ordinated use of the ailerons/wing-warping and the rudder, long, flat, skidding turns were usually attempted. In the afternoon Mr Holder and Granville Bradshaw made low hops, but Dawes continued to be the star of the show.

Two days later he was reported by the *Express and Star* to have 'surprised and surpassed himself' with an inadvertent cross-country flight. The country he inadvertently crossed was reported with due reverence to be some trees, a fence and part of an adjoining field. He had intended to sail round some trees and a house at the western end of the course, but had gone too far and ended up landing in the neighbouring field.

On 17 June Captain Dawes came to grief. After twice circling the racecourse, and reaching a height of 100 ft, as he approached the hangars he swooped down to within a few feet of the ground and then zoomed up in a steep climb. Undoubtedly he stalled the Bleriot and it crashed, smashing one wing, the propeller and the undercarriage, but he stepped from the wreckage unhurt. Low wing-loading and, therefore, slow speeds were to keep many pioneers alive through numerous such accident, not to mention the way the aircraft naturally crumpled up in a crash, absorbing the impact.

Meanwhile Mr Holder had managed to circle the racecourse for the first time, and Granville Bradshaw, happy with his new propeller, was reported to have got his Star off the ground frequently.

Obviously there were those who considered all this excitement would be too much for the ordinary Black Country fellows watching. There was concern expressed in the letters column of the *Express and Star* that there might be trouble at Dunstall Park, if no flying took place. The writer, who signed himself 'Aero', claimed that the general public did not appreciate the difficulties aviators had with even a 20 m.p.h. breeze. He felt that the iron and coal workers of the Black Country, 'the roughest of the rough' as he called them, could only be handled by mounted police, present in some numbers. The Chief Constable was to refute his concern.

In any case, the organizers had made provision for when no flying could take place. The spectator enclosure, along the Gorsebrook Road side of the racecourse, contained two bands and a pierrot troupe to entertain the crowd when the weather was too bad. There were also luncheon and tea tents, and tea-lawns attached to the 5s. and 10s. stands, where tea was served to musical accompaniment.

A large proportion of the early pioneers entered the Dunstall Park Meeting, but not all managed to turn up. S.F. Cody (Aviator's Certificate No. 9) had wanted to come to the Meeting, at least for the appearance money, as he was desperately short of cash, but he crashed his aircraft shortly before and was unable to repair it in time. A.V. Roe was unable to come because he did not have a flyable aircraft ready, and had not yet even gained his Aviator's Certificate. He was to be awarded No. 18, achieved while flying his triplane No. 3 at Brooklands on 26 July. Dunne finally had a practical machine, his D.5, but he chose not to bring it to Wolverhampton.

Arrivals in order of Aviator's Certificate receipt were as follows:

Certificate No. 2, Hon. C.S. Rolls

Charles Rolls, who had recently started a car company with a young engineer named Henry Royce, had long been a famous name in aviation circles, but as a balloonist. When the Wrights' flew in France in 1909 he had been to see their efforts, and had been instrumental in the Short Bros. obtaining a licence to build Wright biplanes, placing an order for two himself, one of which he intended to present to the government.

On 2 June 1910 Rolls became the first man to fly across the Channel both ways. He left Dover at 6.30 p.m. in his Short-Wright and reached Sangatte at 7.10 p.m. where he dropped a letter, and returned to Dover at 8.00 p.m.

News of this flight was carried in the *Express and Star*, which featured a day-by-day build up to the Dunstall Park Meeting. It must have been as eagerly awaited as any event in the town's history. Rolls brought his Short-Wright to Wolverhampton. It was powered by a 35 h.p. Green engine turning a single 7 ft 6 in propeller, rather than the two chain-driven propellers of the normal Wright machine.

After the Dunstall Park Meeting most of the aviators were to make their way almost directly to another aviation meeting at Bournemouth, where tragedy was to strike. On 12 July the Short-Wright of C.S. Rolls broke up in the air, at a height of about 200 ft, and he was killed. He was the first British aviator to die.

Charles Rolls in his Short-Wright biplane, in which he had recently made the first double crossing of the English Channel (Ken Robinson via Jim Boulton)

Certificate No. 3, A. Rawlinson

Another entry was Mr A. Rawlinson, who had recently achieved the doubtful distinction of being the first pilot to be forced down because of the actions of another. In April, at an aviation meeting at Nice, France, he was flying over the sea in his Darraq-powered Farman biplane when a Gnome-powered Farman, flown by a Russian named Effimov, passed so close above him that he was forced down into the water. Effimov was fined 100 francs for his frightful thoughtlessness, but could not have been too upset by this as he won over 77,000 francs at the Meeting, one third of the prize money!

Subsequently Rawlinson had crashed the same Farman at Hendon, and the machine he brought to Wolverhampton was put together from parts of that, and parts of his first machine, which he had flown at Mourmelon in France. The composite was powered by a 60 h.p. ENV engine.

Certificate No. 4, Cecil S. Grace

Cecil Grace arrived with a brand-new Short biplane, having recently shot into the news with a flight over the Fleet at Sheerness. Grace had been flying Short-Wrights at Eastchurch and had co-operated with Short Bros. in the design of the new S.27,

The wreck of A. Rawlinson's Farman, with Graham Gilmour's Farman flying high above, and the Stafford Road works in the background (Ken Robinson via Jim Boulton)

inspired by the Farman, and powered by a 40 h.p. ENV engine. Acting as Shorts' test pilot he took off on the new biplane's first flight, flew to Sheerness and circled some of the navy's battleships. He landed 45 minutes after taking off, having set a new altitude record of 1,180 ft in the process. The three Short brothers were a little tight-lipped over such an adventurous first flight, and the navy was a little alarmed as well, but the S.27 had proved to be very easy to fly.

The subsequent Bournemouth Meeting, Cecil Grace had to remove his French ENV engine because of the all-British rules that applied there, but he was to crash badly, writing-off his aircraft.

Cecil Grace was later to die in December 1910. In an attempt to win a £4,000 prize for the longest flight to the continent, eventually won by T.O.M. Sopwith in a Howard Wright biplane, he crossed the Channel but was forced to stop when he encountered strong head-winds. He landed 2 miles beyond Calais and then set out to return. Apparently under the misconception that Dover was directly north of Calais he was seen by a ship on a course which would have taken him several miles seaward of the North Foreland. He and his aircraft were never seen again. Strangely the ENV engine he had used at Dunstall Park and removed from his aircraft at Bournemouth still survives. It is fitted to a replica of his Short S.27 (the machine he brought to Wolverhampton) at the Cole Palen Museum at Old Rheinbeck, New York.

Certificate No. 5, George Bertram Cockburn

Another Farman arrival was George Bertram Cockburn. He had been the only British entrant at the Rheims meeting of 1909, after only six weeks training in a Gnome-engined Farman at Chalons. Discounting the British-born Henry Farman, who considered himself a Frenchman, Cockburn was the second Briton ever to fly successfully (after Moore-Brabazon), though he did not obtain his Royal Aero Club Certificate (No. 5) until April 1910. His Farman was only the second ever built, and by now was looking quite old and tired. Later he was to train the navy's first aviators at Eastchurch, and became Assistant Manager of the Air Inspection Department at Farnborough, responsible for airframes.

Certificate No. 6, Claude Grahame-White

In April 1910 an almost unknown aviator, Claude Grahame-White, who had recently learned to fly in France, made a valiant attempt to beat the experienced Frenchman, Louis Paulhan, for the London to Manchester prize. In trying bravely to overtake Paulhan he made the first ever night take-off, but could not make up enough time. Nevertheless he became a celebrity overnight, and originally announced his intention

Claude Grahame-White flying along the Birmingham canal, with Oxley Sidings in the background (Ken Robinson via Jim Boulton)

of flying from his hangar at Brooklands to Wolverhampton for the Dunstall Park Meeting, but an accident prevented this.

Grahame-White arrived by train with a brand new Farman, replacing the one he had crashed at Brooklands, and had to employ a gang of men to carry it bodily to Dunstall Park. On 21 May he had flown from Brooklands to Woking police court, where he was fined £5 for speeding in his motor car at Byfleet. One of the magistrates then took him to his house for tea!

Subsequently Grahame-White became arguably the most famous aviator in Great Britain. He founded Hendon Aerodrome, which became a flying Mecca before the First World War, and built up his own aircraft company.

Certificate No. 7, Alec Ogilvie

Alec Ogilvie also brought a new Short-Wright biplane, with which he had been practising at Eastchurch. One of the small coterie of young men attracted to flying, he went on to more serious things in the coming war. With Harris Booth he devised an Airspeed Indicator which went into mass production, and then, in 1915, he became an Admiralty flying instructor. Later on, as a Commander, Ogilvie became head of the Technical Department of the Air Board. In June 1918 he had a lucky escape when flying in the prototype of the giant Handley Page V/1500 four-engined bomber. It crashed and burst into flames, and Ogilvie was the sole survivor, very fortunate to be riding in the tail-gunner's position. Later still, as a Lieutenant-Colonel, Ogilvie resigned his commission and set up his own firm of aviation consultants, Ogilvie & Partners Ltd.

Certificate No. 10, Lt. L.D.L. Gibbs, RFA

In March 1910 Lancelot Gibbs had managed to fly the Dunne D.5, fitted with a 60 h.p. ENV engine. It had been built for Captain Dunne by Shorts at their new factory at Eastchurch, on the Isle of Sheppey. Gibbs had recently set up his own company to give demonstration flights and joy-rides in his own Farman biplane, and he entered this for the Dunstall Park Meeting. He also entered a Sommer biplane, built by Roger Sommer, but with the controls altered to suit Gibbs. Roger Sommer was a wealthy French felt manufacturer, who had flown a Farman at the Rheims Meeting in 1909, and then gone on to build his own aircraft on Farman lines.

Certificate No. 12, James Radley

A Bleriot monoplane was entered by James Radley, who in the next few years was to go on to build several designs of his own, including his 1913 Waterplane, which was a two-hulled flying boat, powered by three Gnome engines driving one propeller. This remarkable machine was capable of carrying six people, three in each hull. A little later in 1910, at the Lanark Flying Meeting, Radley claimed the British speed record by doing

Launcelot Gibbs' Farman. This aircraft, with the ubiquitous 50 h.p. Gnome engine, was the most successful combination of the day and widely copied (Ken Robinson via Jim Boulton)

James Radley (No. 4) in front of his Bleriot, on which he aggregated the most flying at the Meeting for a monoplane, 8 minutes 55 seconds (Wolverhampton Central Library)

75 m.p.h. over a measured mile. As well as his Bleriot he also brought a Macfie Empress biplane to Wolverhampton. The Macfie was one of the least-known types in the country.

Robert Francis Macfie had been born in San Francisco, but came to Great Britain in 1909. Soon afterwards he built his first aircraft at Fambridge Essex, a tractor-monoplane. Macfie was dogged by ill-luck in trying to find a suitable flying ground and this continued with the biplane he built in 1910. Eventually he took it to Brooklands where it made its first flights on 18 June. It was underpowered as the 60 h.p. JAP engine he had ordered had not arrived and he fitted the 35 h.p. JAP taken from the remains of his monoplane. It was altered to Farman configuration and Radley arrived at Wolverhampton with it on 27 June.

Certificate No. 13, Hon. Alan Boyle

The Hon. Alan Boyle arrived with his Howard Wright Avis monoplane. He had gained his Aviator's Certificate just before the Dunstall Park Meeting (14 June at Brooklands). Alan Boyle, like Cecil Grace, was to crash at the next Bournemouth Meeting, in his Howard Wright Avis No. 3, and was badly concussed.

Certificate No. 16, George A. Barnes

An entrant with a Humber-built Bleriot was George Barnes, a well-known local racing motor-cyclist. He had built his own monoplane at Abbey Wood in Kent in 1909. Powered by a 20 h.p. JAP engine it had managed to fly low over the ground for a distance of one and a half miles. He then bought his Humber and gained his Aviator's Certificate No. 16 on 21 June at Brooklands, only a few days before arriving at Wolverhampton.

There were a number of other entries who had still to obtain their Aviator's Certificate, but hoped to do so just prior to the Meeting.

Graham Gilmour

On 28 June Graham Gilmour had flown his Bleriot over the Clyde in front of a reported 35,000 spectators, thereby becoming the first Scotsman to fly in public in Scotland. Strangely, although he did not obtain his Aviator's Certificate, he was allowed to fly at Wolverhampton. Perhaps his newly-found fame meant he could not be left out of the proceedings.

Gilmour was another pilot who died before too long. He was an exuberant, charming and energetic man who became a pilot for the newly-formed British and Colonial Aeroplane Company, and was entered in the Circuit of Britain Air Race of 1911. Unfortunately his licence was suspended for low flying over the Henley Regatta, and he could not take part in the race, much to the displeasure of his employers. On another occasion he had to go to court on a charge of furious driving, but the magistrate was so impressed by the fact that Gilmour flew over to the court in his aircraft that he only gave him a nominal fine!

Subsequently he flew his Bristol Boxkite on pleasure journeys all over England, the first person to indulge in aerial touring. He was killed on 17 February 1912. Flying had been suspended at Brooklands because of the horrid weather, but he still took off in a Martin-Handasyde Dragonfly monoplane, heading for Hendon. His aircraft broke up over Richmond Park.

H.J.D. Astley

A Lane monoplane was entered by H.J.D. Astley. The Lane was designed by Charles Lane at Lane's British Aeroplanes Ltd, of Foley Street, London, and was powered by a 25 h.p. Anzani engine. It was very like a Bleriot, but had a biplane tailplane, the lower part being fixed, and the upper being the elevators. Like the Star it had been exhibited for the first time at the Olympia Aero Show in April. Astley had built his own monoplane the previous year, powered by a 40 h.p. NEC engine, but he obviously thought investing £500 in a Lane was a better bet.

Astley was not to gain his Aviator's Certificate (No. 48) until 24 January 1911, flying a Sommer biplane at Brooklands. Coincidentally Robert Macfie gained his certificate (No. 49) the same day, flying his own biplane, also at Brooklands. Astley later flew a Birdling monolane in the 1911 Circuit of Britain race, without much success.

Capt. George William Patrick Dawes

Capt. Dawes was an army officer who had already served with distinction in the Boer War. He was to join the Royal Flying Corps on its formation in 1912 and commanded the Corps in the Balkans from 1916 to 1918 as an Acting General. In addition to his Queen's Medal with three clasps the King's Medal with two clasps, awarded in South Africa, he was awarded the DSO, the AFC, and was mentioned in despatches seven times. He also received the Croix de Guerre, with three palms, the Serbian Order of the White Eagle, the Order of the Redeemer of Greece, and was created Officer de Legion d'Honneur.

In the Second World War Capt. Dawes served with the Royal Air Force as a Wing Commander, retiring in 1946 with the MBE. In addition to his impressive collection of medals, he had the distinction of being one of the few men to serve in the Boer War and both world wars, and in three different services to boot! For good measure he is also credited with making the first flight on the Indian subcontinent. Surviving his crash at Dunstall Park, and leading such an adventurous life in such a hazardous trade, it is a wonder he managed to reach the age of eighty, dying in March 1960.

Lionel Mander

A Bleriot monoplane was brought to the Meeting by Lionel Mander, of Wolverhampton's famous Mander family. He had taken up flying on the continent, after making a name for himself as a gentleman racing driver.

The Humber company pilot, M Prevateau, was also present but was prevented from

Captain J.H. Cooke and his wife, with presumably their daughter, posing in front of a Bleriot monoplane. It is possibly Lionel Mander's aircraft, Lionel Mander being the Black Country's first pilot (Wolverhampton Central Library)

flying in the Meeting as he was French, and it had been billed as an all-British Meeting. (Although Cecil Grace was Irish-born with an American passport, the other aviators decided to allow him to take part.)

Full list of entrants

Bleriot monoplane	– Capt. Dawes, Lionel Mander, James Radley, Graham Gilmour
Farman biplane	– Claude Grahame-White, A. Rawlinson, George Cockburn, Lancelot Gibbs
Hartill monoplane	– Edgar Hartill
Humber monoplane	– George Barnes, N. Holder

Lane monoplane	– H.J.D. Astley
Macfie Empress	– James Radley (2nd a/c)
Short S.27	– Cecil Grace
Short-Wright biplane	– Charles Rolls, Alec Ogilvie
Roger Sommer biplane	– Lancelot Gibbs (2nd a/c)
Star monoplane	– Granville Bradshaw
Howard Wright Avis	– Alan Boyle

The Dunstall Park course was originally laid out as a triangle of one and one-eighth miles in length, following the shape of the racecourse. At the suggestion of the more experienced pilots it was altered to a diamond shape of one mile, so that the corners were not so sharp. The judge's box was in the centre, and an elaborate system of coloured flags was adopted to tell the spectators what was going on. Qualification for certificates and practice began on the 25th. As a preliminary George Barnes flew round the course, but touched the ground several times.

Captain Dawes, with his rebuilt Bleriot flew twice round the course, and reached a height of 30 ft and a speed of 30 m.p.h. He was duly awarded Aviator's Certificate No. 17, the first serving British army officer to obtain one.

Ignominious failures

Mr Hartill in his own monoplane made two attempts to qualify. On the first his engine did not work well, and he rolled along the course until a spring broke. On the second attempt he once more rolled along the ground until he was level with the judge's box, then the machine buried its nose in the ground, badly damaging it. He was not awarded his pilot's certificate.

Granville Bradshaw was replaced in the pilot's seat of the Star by Mr Lisle of Star Engineering, but he only succeeded in getting it a foot or two off the ground in a short hop. How Granville tried his hand, and went valiantly two or three times round the course, but unfortunately he failed to leave the ground at all!

The start of the Meeting

On the first day of the Meeting the wind was very high and there was no flying for a long while. The machines were paraded in front of the enclosure to give the large crowd something to look at. Then there was a lull and Grahame-White immediately started his engine and took off, carrying a pupil of his named Wickham.

The wind was still high enough to bounce the Farman around, especially as the location of Dunstall Park caused all kinds of eddies, not least round a clump of trees at the western end. Grahame-White landed at the far end of the course, turned his machine round and then flew back.

This encouraged Barnes and Boyle to fly as far as the clump of trees, and then Gibbs tried his Sommer as he did not want to risk his Farman in the poor conditions. He flew low as he was still not used to it, a gust caught him, and he buckled the axle on landing.

Cecil Grace also flew to the top end of the racecourse and then turned and, with the wind behind him, did 60 m.p.h. down the back straight. Radley also did a straight flight to the top of the course, before landing, and when Grace tried another circuit he only passed 6 ft above Radley's head.

In the evening Grahame-White, Radley and Rawlinson all made further straight flights, but the following day there was almost no flying at all, as it was blowing a gale. Alec Ogilvie tried a flight at 4.30 a.m. before the wind really increased, and before the official start, but he made a heavy landing and broke a wire and a skid.

The 'get off' competition

Wednesday was better and the 'get-off' competition was attempted in between heavy rain showers. Radley, and Gibbs in his Farman both failed to qualify in early attempts as they did not fly at least 200 yards after their take-off. Rawlinson set the standard with a take-off run of only 100 ft 5 in, which was to win him the £100. This was the first prize ever won by a British subject in a flying competition restricted to British nationals. Grahame-White came second with a run of 101 ft 7 in on the second of three attempts, and of the others only Barnes and Boyle tried their luck, Boyle buckling a wheel of his Avis when he landed. Radley and Gibbs flew complete circuits before the rain set in again.

Duration flying

After 7.30 p.m. the competition for the longest duration aggregate was able to begin. Rawlinson flew for just over 7 minutes but then he tipped on one side in landing and buckled the wing of the Farman. Grahame-White flew for just over 15 minutes and then Grace did a splendid flight of 27 minutes 45 seconds, reaching a height of 500 ft, and flying out over the railway line at one point. Finally Rolls, Radley, Dawes and Barnes all did short flights before flying ceased.

Thursday opened with yet more rain, and the course was becoming a quagmire in places with deep ruts. There was no flying until 8 p.m. at which point Boyle and Radley both managed a circuit. Then Gibbs, Grace and Grahame-White for a long while were all in the air together. Grace stayed up for 24 minutes and the other two for 30 minutes each.

On Friday 25,000 spectators turned up, but yet again there was no flying because of the inclement weather. Saturday morning dawned with even worse conditions. There was thunder and lightning, pouring rain, and hailstorms; in other words, typical English summer weather!

Also typically, there was a miraculous clearing of the skies in the afternoon, and the wind dropped enough for flying to begin. Lancelot Gibbs had his Farman biplane

Aviators and others, no doubt discussing the appalling weather. Third from left James Radley, fourth from left Claude Grahame-White, fifth from left G.S. Stubbs, and on the right Captain J.H. Cooke (Wolverhampton Central Library)

wheeled out of the hangar, and started his 50 h.p. Gnome rotary. He rolled forward, and soon there was a shout of 'He's up!' from the excited crowd. For half an hour he circled the course, adding to his time for the aggregate duration prize.

Alan Boyle flew his Howard Wright monoplane on a 3 minute flight which reached a height of 80 ft as he sailed over the treetops. Then Cecil Grace took to the air, followed immediately by Grahame-White. As the wind freshened again, Grace was blown slightly off course and had to land in a nearby field, damaging his propeller, but Grahame-White flew on.

Alan Boyle returned to the air, but very shortly he too was blown off course and landed heavily near to Grace's aircraft. James Radley tried his luck in his Bleriot, but after only 200 yards he crashed, stepping unhurt from the wreckage. His Macfie biplane had been damaged by the weather and so he had been unable to use that.

Now Alec Ogilvie took off in his Short-Wright, never an easy aircraft to fly, because of its basic instability, often displayed by its undulating flight. He was caught by a gust of wind, and forced down to a heavy landing.

Grahame-White landed after half an hour, and rain began falling again, curtailing flying for a while. By 8 p.m. it had stopped and Lancelot Gibbs, Charles Rolls, and Claude Grahame-White were all soon in the air together. It was said to be a beautiful sight, the three frail biplanes flying together round the course against a background of the setting sun.

It was probably a fitting climax to the Meeting, but as a moment of beauty it was all too brief. Gibbs must have flown into the propeller wash of one of the other two, the hazards of which were not fully appreciated, and his machine crashed heavily. An eyewitness said the crash scene looked like 'a Gnome engine standing on the ground with splinters of wood all around it'.

Rolls landed after a short while, but Grahame-White continued for 15 minutes until he had surpassed Gibbs' aggregate total, so winning the £1,000 prize. His total flying time had been 1 hour 23 minutes 20 seconds, and Gibbs won the second prize of £200 with a total of 1 hour 13 minutes 5 seconds, but he must have been bitterly disappointed as he was holding the lead when he crashed. He lodged an objection, but later withdrew it.

First ten placings in this category were:

			hour	min.	sec.
1.	C. Grahame-White	(Farman)	1	23	20
2.	Lt. L. Gibbs	(Farman)	1	13	5
3.	C. Grace	(Short S.27)		55	43
4.	A. Ogilvie	(Short-Wright)		9	19
5.	J. Radley	(Bleriot)		8	55
6.	C.S. Rolls	(Short-Wright)		8	35
7.	G. Barnes	(Humber)		8	19
8.	A. Boyle	(Howard Wright)		7	53
9.	A. Rawlinson	(Farman)		7	36
10.	G. Gilmour	(Bleriot)		7	5

The Earl of Plymouth's Trophy for the fastest three circuits of the course was won by C.S. Rolls in a time of 4 minutes 13 seconds, 6 seconds faster than Grahame-White could manage. James Radley won the separate prize for monoplanes, and George Barnes carried off the honours for the members of the Midland Aero Club. Several competitions had to be cancelled, including those for passenger flying and figure flying.

It was perhaps surprising that Captain Dawes had not figured more prominently in the prizes, having made such sterling progress in the preceding weeks, but it is likely that there was something wrong with his machine.

There have to be winners and losers in any contest, and at Dunstall Park Granville

Bradshaw was one of the losers. Subsequently Granville designed a 40 h.p. four-cylinder in-line engine for the Howard Flanders B.2 biplane which was built at Brooklands. The B.2 had been designed to take a promised 100 h.p. V8 from ABC, but that did not materialize, and it flew remarkably well on half the power. Bradshaw also designed the two-cylinder, air-cooled ABC Gnat which produced 45 h.p. from 3.2 litres, and powered a few Sopwith Sparrows early in the war, but he was to go on to mightier things, designing a series of air-cooled static radials. This series began with the 110 h.p. Mosquito, of little practical value, continued with the 170 h.p. Wasp, and finishing with the 320 h.p. Dragonfly, which was one of the biggest fiascos ever inflicted on British aviation, but more of that later.

The Meeting had been a mixed success, ruined largely by the weather. It did not have the cachet of being the first, as did Doncaster in the previous year, but it was a brave effort by Wolverhampton, much anticipated, and much remembered. Certainly the railway workers in Oxley Sidings, who had a grandstand view of the proceedings, were to remember it long afterwards. One of them was my grandfather.

Those at Dunstall Park who were soon to die, Charles Rolls, Cecil Grace and Graham Gilmour, represented the rich adventurers who took to flying as their contemporaries took to car-racing. Their spirit helped to bring flying to the forefront of the nation's conscience. The serious innovators like Cody, Alliott Verdon Roe, and Howard Wright helped prepare Britain's aviation industry for the more serious matters that were to come.

6

1910, ACCLES & POLLOCK'S *MAYFLY*, OLDBURY

Lt. John Seddon's aircraft, which had been entered for the Dunstall Park Meeting, was finally completed later in the year. He called it the *Mayfly*, an optimistic name if ever there was one, and its image became one of the most famous in the aviation world. Whenever photographs of weird and wonderful flying machines have been collected Seddon's *Mayfly* is inevitably included.

Seddon had become interested in aviation in 1908 when a fellow officer had demonstrated a paper model aircraft with a tandem-wing layout, reminiscent of the Langley Aerodrome. Convinced that steel tube was lighter and stronger than wood, he determined to build an aircraft with this material. It was perhaps inevitable that he should turn to Accles & Pollock of Oldbury to build it, with their great experience of manipulating steel tube.

Walter Hackett, then Managing Director of Accles & Pollock, helped design the aircraft, and his brother, Alfred Hackett, designed the clips, landing gear, engine mountings and the very complicated control mechanism.

The fore and aft biplane wings were supported on 12 ft diameter, crossed hoops of 2 in steel tubing, of varying gauges, and the engines were carried between them within further hoops. It had the appearance of barbed wire entanglements, or spiral doodles from a designer's blotter. The front wing surfaces were also supposed to act as elevators, with the rear ones just providing lift. The span was 50 ft giving an immense wing area of about 1,000 sq. ft. It was also about 50 ft long.

The *Mayfly* had two New Engine Co. 65 h.p. engines, built by Mort Bros. of Acton, mounted side by side between the fore and aft wings, driving aluminium propellers. It had 2,000 feet of tubing and not surprisingly weighed about a ton, not including the pilot and the five passengers it was supposed to carry. If the engines could have been persuaded to give their full design power of 130 h.p. the power-to-weight ratio would have been fairly low for the time, even though it was almost certainly the heaviest aircraft built up to then. But it appears that the two engines were never made to run at the same time.

The *Mayfly* was towed on its own wheels the 12 miles to Dunstall Park by horse, and must have caused some amazement along the route, which was via Sedgeley. When the big day arrived for the first trial, the starboard engine was started, but the port engine took ten minutes before it would fire, and when the starboard engine was opened up, it stopped and had to be sent back to Mort Bros. for repair.

The Accles & Pollock-built Seddon *Mayfly* at Dunstall Park. A confusing construction of steel hoops, it would have been the biggest aircraft in the world, but it did not have the slightest chance of flying (Accles & Pollock)

After a fortnight's wait another attempt was made, but this time the port engine broke down. After ten more days a third attempt was made, but one of the propellers broke up. Next, one of the chains that drove the propellers broke, and then an engine broke down again. On a trial run on 7 November an axle collapsed under the weight. This catalogue of disasters was to finally frustrate the *Mayfly*'s attempts to fly. The navy could no longer tolerate Seddon's absence from his duties, and he was recalled.

As well as becoming part of aviation history because of its surreal shape, the *Mayfly* was actually the first all-metal aircraft ever built, and the largest aircraft built up to that time. It also qualifies as the first example of modern sculpture. Despite its name it never really had a hope of flying, because it was built to far too low a safety factor of 2 to 1, and if its engines could ever have been made to work properly, it would have suffered from continual structural failures.

After being picked apart by souvenir hunters the remains ended up in a scrapyard. Seddon managed to get himself transferred to Eastchurch as the fifth naval officer to learn to fly. His lack of understanding of aircraft control is shown by the fact that on his first solo he still had the idea fixed in his mind that it was necessary to push right in order to turn left. After a tolerable right-hand circuit, instead of the left-hand one he had intended, he landed with his right wing too near the hangars. In attempting to turn left, he turned right, and crashed into them!

His flying improved, but this episode throws further doubt on the likelihood of the *Mayfly* ever flying. He was later awarded the Britannia Trophy for the best flight of the year, for a flight in a Maurice Farman seaplane from the Isle of Grain to Plymouth to search for a missing submarine. Shortly afterwards he flew Winston Churchill from Gravesend to Grain in a Short seaplane, into the teeth of a gale, a much publicized flight.

Jack Seddon became a Commander during the First World War and the first Chief of the Navy's Experimental Construction Department.

7

1910–14, FURTHER FLYING AT DUNSTALL, WOLVERHAMPTON

The company that had been set up to run the 1910 Meeting, Midlands Aviation Syndicate Ltd, had to be wound up. The expenditure of £4,711 9s. 9d. had been £552 13s. less than income. The largest costs were for the prizes, which totalled £1,896 10s. and the hangars, which had cost £615 15s. 4d.

Four aircraft remained at Dunstall after the Meeting, Preveteau's Humber, Bradshaw's Star, Seddon's Tandem biplane and Holder's Bleriot. Holder crashed his aircraft in the week after the Meeting but he was unhurt.

The Star monoplane was tested again in October without any more success. During the later part of the year Star built a biplane roughly of Farman configuration, and this was completed by November, but there is no record of it having flown.

In 1911 the monoplane was radically modified. The strange tailplane was replaced with a conventional rudder and elevators, but no fixed fin was retained. Rounded wing-tips replaced the earlier square cut ones, and the span was reduced from 42 ft to 37 ft. The height of the wing-bracing pylon was increased and the undercarriage strengthened. A more powerful Star engine, giving 50 h.p. was fitted. It has been reported that in this version the Star monoplane made one flight in the hands of Joseph Lisle, one of Edward Lisle's sons, but his father was so alarmed at the sight of his son up in the air that he banned all further aeronautical work by the company!

The modified Star monoplane at Dunstall Park in 1911, with a conventional tail. It was in this form that it is said to have made its only flight (D.C. Hunt)

The aircraft was dismantled and the engine was sold to a gentleman who fitted it to an ornithopter, which as in the case of all such devices, was entirely unsuccessful. Remarkably the engine still survives, in the hands of the Royal Air Force Museum, Hendon.

Mann & Overtons monoplane

Another aircraft was also tested late in 1910 at Dunstall Park. Mann & Overtons Ltd, coachbuilders of Pimlico, had built a monoplane on Demoiselle lines that they exhibited at Olympia earlier in the year. It was powered by a 35 h.p. Anzani engine, and had a span of 18 ft 4 in and a length of 20 ft. The fuselage frame was made of steel tubing. The flight trials were extremely unsuccessful.

Possibly Mann & Overtons (and other Demoiselle imitators like Edgar Hartill) had failed to take into account the fact that Santos Dumont, the designer and pilot of the successful Demoiselle was a very small and lightweight man. Certainly when a flying Demoiselle replica was built many years later for the film *Those Magnificent Men in their Flying Machines*, despite using an efficient modern engine they still had to use one of the lightest women pilots they could find, Joan Hughes, to get it off the ground. Even then it was only marginally capable of flight, and had to be fitted with larger wings and a 50 h.p. engine for practical use in the film.

An unknown aircraft at Dunstall Park. It looks a little like a 1910 Deperdussin, and may be a copy. The engine is a V4 (Jim Boulton)

It is very easy to sympathize with Edgar Hartill, and the Mann & Overtons pilot as they trundled manfully round Dunstall Park without much hope at all of daylight ever appearing under the wheels. High hopes that were dashed, but might have been realized if only they had chosen to copy the Bleriot or the Farman instead of the Demoiselle.

By airship to Birmingham

In March 1911 Ernest Willows brought his airship, *City of Cardiff*, to Dunstall Park. A Welshman, Willows had built the first practical all-British airship in Cardiff, Spencer's airship being little more than a powered balloon, incapable of flying against a wind. Willows' airship was powered by a 30 h.p., eight-cylinder JAP engine, and it flew for the first time on 5 September 1905. He was only nineteen years old, but was encouraged and supported by his father. His second airship, which was of 21,000 cu. ft capacity, twice as large as the previous one, first flew on 26 November 1909, and in July 1910 he flew it from Cardiff to London non-stop. The 140 miles he covered in 10 hours was the longest flight at that time by a British airship.

His third airship was of 32,000 cu. ft capacity and was powered by the same JAP engine, driving two propellers, and he named it *City of Cardiff*. It first flew on 29 October 1910, and in November he made the first flight from London to Paris by a British subject, though it was in two stages. After crossing the Channel he had to land when darkness fell, and was promptly presented with an import-tax bill by a French Customs officer, for the gas he had 'imported'!

He had ideas of setting up a factory to make airships in Wolverhampton. In April 1910 a local syndicate had been formed to assist him in this, and a large shed to hold the *City of Cardiff* was planned to be built for him at Dunstall Park. Sufficient financial support was not forthcoming however.

During March 1911 he had wanted to fly from Watford – where he had been displaying the airship – to Wolverhampton, but high winds forced him to bring it by rail, and then prevented him from inflating it for several days. He had brought a hangar with him, which was assembled during the last two weeks of March.

On 31 March he was finally able to fill it with 32,000 cu. ft of hydrogen in the yard of the Knowles Oxygen Company in Wolverhampton. At just after 3.30 p.m. he took off and flew across Whitmore Reans to Dunstall Park, alighting in the centre of the racecourse. After photographs were taken the *City of Cardiff* was moved into the hangar.

On the afternoon of Saturday 1 April the weather was fine with only a light easterly breeze and the airship was brought from the hangar. After a delay while further photographs were taken he did two circuits of the racecourse carrying his mechanic. He then alighted to discharge ballast before taking off again for a flight to Birmingham.

There were very few spectators, but after circling a few times to gain height, the ones present gave him a cheer as he set course. The Honorary Secretary of the Midland Aero Club, Gilbert Dennison, set off in a car with a white flag spread over to lead the way. The pale yellow airship circled the town centre, and large crowds gathered to watch before he flew away.

The Willows airship at Dunstall Park. The figures to the right of the little boy are Gilbert Dennison (Secretary of the Midland Aero Club), E.T. Willows, Mr Leo Harris, Mr Knowles of Knowles Oxygen Co. (who had filled the airship with hydrogen), Captain J.H. Cooke, Mrs Willows, Mrs Dennison, and Mrs Cooke (D.C. Hunt)

He reached the Walsall area by 2.20 p.m., but a feed pipe uncoiled between Walsall and Perry Barr and he landed to effect a repair. Taking off again he circled Dennison's house in Handsworth Wood before heading for Birmingham city centre.

He circled the Town Hall and the Council House at between 600 and 900 ft, and dropped a few of his visiting cards. The return journey to Dunstall took 35 minutes and he landed at 3.45 p.m. He told a reporter from the *Express and Star*, that he had 'had a very nice little trip indeed'.

In the evening he made three local flights carrying single passengers, and the following day he took his wife and Mrs Dennison for a 20 minute flight, which was Mrs Dennison's first. After that there was further bad weather that curtailed his flying, and he deflated his airship on 8 April.

On 17 May he again flew to Birmingham, and having given up the idea of operating from Wolverhampton, he registered his company, E.T. Willows Ltd in Birmingham and based his airship at Castle Bromwich.

His first product was the *Alpha*, a 50,000 cu. ft balloon. On 10 July he brought it to Dunstall Park for a trial trip, taking three passengers. Though it was his first flight in a balloon he crossed the Welsh mountains and landed near Aberystwyth! He later made a number of other flights from Wolverhampton carrying fare-paying passengers.

E.T. Willows, like his contemporary Stanley Spencer, is now almost completely forgotten, but he was one of the most important British airship pioneers, and has been described as the Father of British Airships. His airships were more practical than

Two views of the 18,000 cu. ft balloon *Bee* being inflated with hydrogen at the Knowles Oxygen Co., Wolverhampton, in April 1912. At the same time the 50,000 cu. ft *Meteor* was being inflated with coal gas at Dunstall Park, about a mile and a half away. The two balloons, each with two people on board then took off together and flew to Bridgnorth, where they were tethered for the night. The following day the dual journey continued and ended at Abergavenny, 60 miles away. The cost of the hydrogen in the *Bee* was £4 10s., and the coal gas even less (D.C. Hunt)

Spencer's, which could not fly against even the lightest breeze, but had the cachet of being first. Willows used hydrogen instead of the coal gas which Spencer used, which meant he could use a smaller envelope for the same degree of lift.

Willows' next airship was bought by the Admiralty and became RNAS Airship No. 2, and he helped develop many of the dirigibles used in the First World War. He died in 1926 at a Flower Show in Bedford when the netting of a captive balloon he was flying broke, and the basket fell to the ground.

Aerobatics by Benny Hucks

The Midland Aero Club had also secured the use of land at Castle Bromwich for an airfield. B.C. Hucks had flown from there in 1911, giving passenger flights. On 10 September 1911 he became the first man to fly the Bristol Channel, flying his Blackburn Mercury monoplane from Weston to Cardiff. The following year he toured the Midlands, sponsored by the *Daily Mail*. In 1913, at the request of the Midland Aero Club, he made a series of demonstration flights at Dunstall Park.

Benny Hucks, a Welshman, and a friend of Willows, had acted as Grahame-White's mechanic, in return for a few flying lessons. At the Blackpool Flying Meeting of 1910 he met Robert Blackburn, and in January 1911 joined him at Filey, helping with some of the test-flying which took place on Filey beach. He was so good he soon took over all the test-flying of the Blackburn Mercury monoplane, even before he had obtained his flying certificate!

After the Olympia Aero Show of that year he managed to gain his certificate (No. 91) at Filey, but only just. On completing the last figure of eight the front bearing of the Isaacson radial engine seized, the prop-shaft sheared, and the prop flew off. The aircraft side-slipped into the ground, but Hucks was not badly hurt. Robert Blackburn immediately replaced the Isaacson with a 50 h.p. Gnome.

In July 1911 Hucks was to pilot one of two Blackburn Mercuries in the Circuit of Britain Race, but he nearly wrecked his aircraft just before the race. He hit a ridge on Filey sands and the Mercury stood on its nose. Hucks was thrown out of his seat, as seat-belts were unheard of, and must have been very grateful that he had sand to land in. Only the prop was seriously damaged and Hucks was able to start the race from Brooklands. He completed several stages but engine failure resulted in a forced landing near Luton.

He obtained his own Bleriot to give demonstration flights, and usually kept it at the newly opened Hendon airfield. He became a star at Hendon flying in weekend races, which drew huge crowds.

Unfortunately he did not attract such crowds at Dunstall Park, and the lack of interest shown by club members in particular, was very disappointing. The very continuation of the club was discussed and its undertakings were severely limited for over a year. Then the First World War broke out and all operations were suspended until August 1924.

It is interesting to note how something that had been sensational only three years before, now caused so little interest. In a way it echoed the plummet in the public's interest in the Apollo Moon landings so many years later. When Apollo 11 first landed on the Moon the whole world held its breath, but by the time the last landing was made, by Apollo 17, hardly anyone even noticed.

Benny Hucks went on to become the first Englishman to loop the loop, a manoeuvre which returned the public's interest for a while. He had seen the Frenchman Adolphe Pegoud perform the manoeuvre at Brooklands, and was determined to become the first Englishman to emulate the feat. He went to Buc in France to learn it, and other aerobatics, performing it for the first time on 13 November 1913.

When he demonstrated the loop at Birmingham in February 1914 over 20,000 people turned up to watch. He even painted roundels on the upper surface of his Bleriot's wings so that the watching crowd would know when he was upside-down. During the war Hucks test-flew de Havilland aircraft and invented the famous Hucks Starter. He died in 1918, from pneumonia after a bout of the influenza which swept the country. Considering he was an aviator in such dangerous times it was an unlucky end.

Dunstall Park never did become an aviation centre like Eastchurch, Brooklands or Hendon, but for one brief flowering year or so it had become one of the main airfields in the country. Perhaps if Star Engineering had taken up aircraft manufacture, and Willows had built his airships there after all, things might have been different.

Flying did not cease entirely, though. Nowadays, when someone wants to land a helicopter in Wolverhampton, Dunstall Park is the logical place to choose. In 1988, when I watched from the other side of the canal as a Queen's Flight Wessex carrying Prince Charles landed there, I thought of my grandfather seventy-eight years before, watching the flying from just behind where I stood. Things had come full circle, Dunstall Park was Wolverhampton's first flying field, and now it had become its last: horse-racing permitting.

8

1910, THE FOLEY BIPLANE, STOURBRIDGE

Before the 1910 Flying Meeting at Dunstall Park, aviation had little impact on the Black Country, apart, that is, from the many balloon flights, Spencer's airship flights at Stourbridge and Cody's brief appearance with his man-lifting kites. As with the rest of the country however, Bleriot's Channel crossing and the spur of other achievements by the French pioneers created a burst of interest in heavier-than-air flying, and numerous adventurous men began the construction of flying machines.

In 1910 J.S. Foley of the famous Foley family of Stourbridge designed a pusher biplane and had it built by Mr F.W. Baker of Baker & Co. It had biplane elevators forward of the wing, in the style of the Farman and was powered by an All English 40 h.p. engine. The span was 35 ft and the length 40 ft; the wing area was 360 sq. ft and the weight 600 lb. The design embraced quite a number of patents in the control systems.

Foley had announced his intention of entering for the Dunstall Park Meeting but by 25 June the engine had still not been delivered, and a fortnight's work was still left to do, so he could not attend. There is no record of the Foley biplane ever flying, but that is not to say it never did.

9

1911, THE WALTER DAVIES GLIDERS, DUDLEY

In 1911 Walter Davies of Dudley constructed a biplane glider. Davies had been born in Springmere, Dudley in 1891 and went to Holly Hall School. He had an inventive turn of mind and the glider was totally designed and built by himself.

It had unequal wing spans, the upper being 30 ft and the lower 20 ft. It had a biplane tail, and ailerons set mid-way between the wings. On 27 May 1911 he made the first flight with his glider on the Cavalry Field at the Priory. He glided for some distance and reached a height above the ground of 12 ft.

Two years later he built another glider, which he called his Davies No. 2. This one had a span of 30 ft 1 in and a length of 20 ft 1 in, a wing area of 285 sq. ft and a loaded weight of 285 lb. In September 1913 he tested this one at Lapal, Halesowen. His partner in this venture was S. Bray of the Halesowen Electric Picture Palace.

During the First World War Davies was to be associated with the Sam Summerfield School of Flying on Bisley Common, Birmingham, where he taught among others a group of Chinese students to fly. Later he was employed in the design office of the Bournemouth Aviation Company where one of his designs was a Caudron-type trainer powered by a 80 h.p. Anzani engine. In May 1917 it reached a height of 7,500 ft with one passenger.

After the war he turned to inventing air-screw driven boats, with twin hulls to skim the water. His hydrogliders proved capable of passing up the Severn when the water was far too shallow for boats with screws. He worked for fifty years on such designs, with little official interest, but his work foreshadowed the design of Malcolm Campbell's *Bluebird*.

In the Second World War Davies designed a ground trainer for ATC Squadrons. It was a simple wooden aircraft with a 24 ft span, with all control systems working, and power from a 749 c.c. engine. A prototype was built by 223 ATC Squadron at Halesowen, being completed in March 1942. Plans for the Davies Trainer went to ATC Squadrons all over the country, and also to Australia.

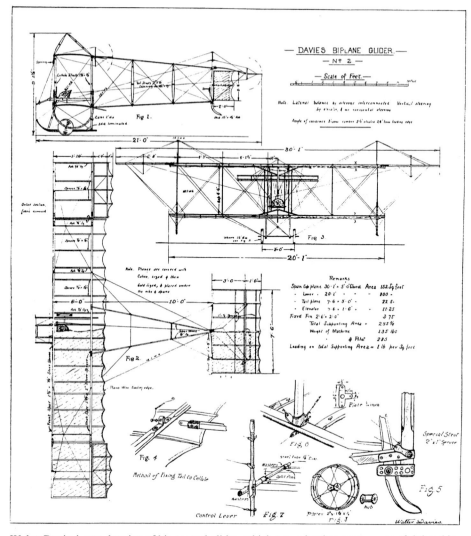

Walter Davies' own drawing of his second glider, which proved rather more successful than his first (D.C. Hunt)

10

1911, THE FLYING SUBMARINE, WOLVERHAMPTON

A Wolverhampton man, Charles Wynwood, caused a stir when he exhibited a model of an all-metal flying boat at the 1911 Aero Show at Olympia. It was an aluminium high-wing monoplane, with a boat-type hull, and would be powered by a 100 h.p. Gnome engine. The engine would drive a large tractor propeller when the machine was in the air, and two smaller propellers, either side of the rear fuselage, when it was in the water, with the wings stowed. The full-size machine would be 50 ft long with a span of 40 ft, and would carry up to twelve passengers within its fuselage.

This amazing futuristic design came to nothing, of course, but though this concept was well ahead of its time it was as nothing compared to Mr Wynwood's future plans for it. He intended to develop it into a submarine, as well as a flying boat and motor launch! This flying submarine foreshadowed *Supercar*, the *Thunderbirds* and various James Bond modes of transport!

11
1913, THE GREAT AIR RACE AT WALSALL

Although a Walsall man, Ernest Maund, had built a monoplane at Craven Arms in Shropshire, an aircraft did not arrive in Walsall itself until 30 September 1913. An air race had been arranged between Benny Hucks and Gustav Hamel, one of the most well-known pilots of the day.

It was sponsored by the Birmingham *Daily Post*, who offered a prize of £500 and a trophy to the winner. The course was 80 miles long, stretching from the Tally Ho grounds in Edgbaston, via Redditch, Coventry, Nuneaton, Tamworth, Walsall, and Quinton, back to Edgbaston. The control point at Walsall was to be on Spring Vale Farm on the Birmingham Road, which was also a refuelling stop.

Gustav Hamel signing for the Royal Mail on the occasion of the first airmail flight in Great Britain (D.C. Hunt)

B.C. Hucks flying his Bleriot monoplane at Hendon. This was the aircraft in which he raced Gustav Hamel, and in which he gave flying demonstrations all over the country, attracting large crowds, especially after he became the first British pilot to loop (D.C. Hunt)

Tremendous interest was generated in Walsall and thousands of people flocked to the area, with a special compound constructed for the mayor and other notables. Hucks and Hamel had both originally intended to fly 80 h.p. two-seat Bleriots, but Hamel damaged his at Hendon just before the race, and flew up in a 80 h.p. Morane-Saulnier monoplane. As this was a faster machine he agreed to take his mechanic with him as a handicap.

With over 20,000 spectators waiting in fervent anticipation, the two airmen arrived within a few seconds of one another. After circling the field Hamel landed first, but Hucks did not see some telegraph wires that ran down one side. At the last second he just managed to swoop underneath them, and soon both planes were surrounded by excited people.

After a stop of about half an hour, the crowd was cleared from the field and the two aircraft took off for Edgbaston once more. Hamel won the race by a margin of only 4.28 seconds.

Aircraft were soon to come to other Black Country towns, but in very different circumstances. Friendly sporting contests were to be replaced by the dread detonation of airborne bombs, as aviation brought war to the British civilian population for the first time since 1745.

12

1914–29, SUNBEAM AERO-ENGINES AND AIRCRAFT, WOLVERHAMPTON

By 1914 aircraft manufacture had progressed in only half a dozen years from the one- and two-man workshops such as those of Howard Wright and A.V. Roe, feeling their way by trial and error, to a significant industry, with large companies, such as Shorts and British & Colonial, producing aircraft in substantial numbers. Existing Black Country firms, specialized as they were in metalwork, were anxious to become involved in the new opportunities that were thus presented.

In 1913 the output of the Sunbeam Car Company of Wolverhampton was the third largest in the country, and they began to look into the possibility of producing aero-engines, perhaps inspired by a government competition to find a suitable British aero-engine, with excellent prizes and the promise of large orders offered. Their Chief Engineer was Louis Coatalen, a Frenchman who had previously worked for Humber in Coventry. In 1913 he had produced an advanced racing engine featuring twin overhead camshafts and four valves per cylinder, but the first aero-engine he designed featured the side valves of Sunbeam's touring cars.

It was the V8 Crusader that developed 150 h.p. from 7.6 litres. Another engine of 100 h.p., most likely just a version of the Crusader, was built at the start of the war, but only seven appear to have been delivered, and they were never named. They may have powered two Sopwith Type 806 Gunbuses.

The names of Sunbeam engines were mostly those of various tribes from around the world, but the system of naming them did not begin immediately. In the beginning they were usually referred to by their horse-power; thus the Crusader may not have ever been referred to by its name while it was in production, the name being applied retrospectively, after a Ministry of Munitions memo on the subject in 1917. The names of the various engines are used throughout to avoid confusion with other Sunbeam engines of the same horse-power.

Sunbeam Crusader 150 h.p.

Sunbeam purchased a Farman biplane in which to test the Crusader and other designs. The effect on the handling of the Farman, replacing its little 50 h.p. Gnome with a 600 lb, 150 h.p. engine, must have been interesting, and one wonders how well the structure survived. Test flying took place at Brooklands and Shoreham, and the aircraft took part in the 1914 London–Manchester Air Race. The pilot engaged to fly the

Sunbeam's first aero-engine, the side valve V-8, which was later named Crusader (D. Griffiths)

aircraft was John Alcock, who was later to become more well known with his name coupled to that of Arthur Whitten Brown – Alcock and Brown were the first people to fly the Atlantic non-stop, in their Vickers Vimy.

With war approaching and very little in the way of a British aero-engine industry, the Royal Naval Air Service turned to Sunbeam in particular to produce the engines that would be needed. In February 1914 the War Office purchased a Crusader which was tested at Farnborough for several months and was considered to the first modern British aero engine purchased by the Royal Aircraft Factory.

A Crusader was fitted to one of James Radley's aircraft, the Radley-England Waterplane No. 2. In 1914 Radley and E. Gordon England rebuilt their first Waterplane, following a crash, and replaced the three 50 h.p. Gnomes, with which it was powered, by a single Crusader, intending to enter it in the Circuit of Britain Air Race. Unfortunately they had a great deal of trouble with the engine and the aircraft never flew.

The Crusader was later fitted to the Sopwith Gunbus, replacing a 100 h.p. Monosoupape engine. Some of these served with the RNAS at Dunkirk in the early months of the war, and a total of thirty-six were fitted with Crusaders.

The first commercial application of a Sunbeam aero-engine. The Radley-England twin-hulled waterplane fitted with the 150 h.p. Crusader, replacing three 50 h.p. Gnomes (D. Griffiths)

A Russian heavy bomber

It was also fitted to the world's first heavy bomber the Russian Ilya Mouretmetz. This had first flown in 1913, fitted with four German Argus engines, but with the outbreak of war and a chronic shortage of aero-engines, a variety were fitted to the eighty production IMs. Thirty Crusaders were sent to Russia and fitted to the Mark V version of the IM, one with a 97 ft 8 in wing span, weighing 6,950 lb empty, and armed with two machine guns. They gave it a top speed of 75 m.p.h. at 6,500 ft, and were the least liked engines available. The Russians preferred Argus, Salmson, Renault or even their own RBVZ engines to the Crusaders. The fact that they were made available at all probably means the Air Ministry held them in little esteem once better engines had become available in Britain. The Ilya Mouretmetz-equipped units became the élite of the Russian Air Service, and the type was highly successful, dropping over 2,300 bombs, and only losing one of their number to German fighter attack.

The Crusader was also installed in the Short Type 827 seaplane, an initial order of twelve being placed in mid-1914, and the Crusader eventually powered 108 of them. (Not the Sunbeam Nubian as is often suggested, the last Type 827 was built before the first Nubian was delivered.)

The Crusader was later fitted to the Coastal class of non-rigid airship, each having two engines one at each end of the car, which was actually two Avro 510 fuselages joined together. These gave the Coastals a duration of 11 hours at their full speed of 42 knots. At least eighteen of the twenty-four Coastals built had Sunbeam engines. This association with airships was to be a feature of the company.

Sunbeam Mohawk 225 h.p.

Coatalen enlarged the Crusader to produce a V12 giving 225 h.p. from 11.4 litres, and it was called the Mohawk. One of the first applications for the Mohawk was the Sopwith Bat Boat No. 2, which was constructed for the 1914 Round Britain Race, but because of the war the race did not take place. Another competitor for this race was the Avro 510, and this was also powered by the Mohawk.

An even more spectacular projected use for the Mohawk was the Martin-Handasyde Transatlantic Monoplane. Built to win the *Daily Mail*'s £10,000 prize for the first flight across the Atlantic it was a 66 ft span, two-seat monoplane, of fairly conventional design, even using wing-warping instead of ailerons. It was nearly completed in May 1914 when the projected pilot, Gustav Hamel, who had been the first pilot to land in Walsall, was killed, and events in Serbia ended all hopes that the attempt would take place.

All too quickly flying had become no longer just a sport and an adventure. Flying had become a very serious business indeed.

The First World War

At the beginning of the war Britain did not have an aero-engine factory worthy of the name. French engines were the primary power units of most aircraft and they were manufactured under licence. The War Office looked to motor car manufacturers in particular to produce French engines and to come up with designs of their own.

Short 827 seaplane

The Sunbeam Car Company not only expanded its aero-engine manufacturing at the start of the war, it also began to build aircraft under licence. Of a total of 108 Crusader-powered Short 827s built, 40 were constructed by Sunbeam itself. Short seaplanes, powered by Sunbeam engines, were to be engaged in a number of notable actions.

The attack on the *Graf von Goetzen*

Three Mohawk-powered 827s engaged in one of the little-known sideshows of the war, on Lake Tanganyika. The Germans on the eastern side of the lake had created two powerful warships – the *Graf von Goetzen* and the *Hedwig von Wisman* – with which they shelled the Belgian positions on the other side of the lake with impunity. The Belgians improvised a naval force and managed to sink the *Hedwig von Wisman*, but in late 1915 they called for help from the British Admiralty to sink the other German warship.

They had no seaplanes of their own and the British sent them three Sunbeam-built Short 827s powered by Crusader engines. The aircraft, associated equipment and Belgian pilots came overland from the River Congo, and set up base on Lake Tongwe, quite near to Lake Tanganyika. The first Short was ready to fly on 13 May 1916. The main target, the *Graf von Goetzen*, was in Kigoma harbour on the other side of the lake, 165 miles away.

On 10 June, after a few mishaps because of the weather and engine trouble, Lieutenant Orta set off for Kigoma with two 65 lb bombs on board. For the last

10 miles he dropped down to 500 ft, and when still 2 miles from the harbour the warship began firing at him. He dropped his two little bombs one of which fell short, but the other hit the stern of the ship.

On the way back he developed engine trouble and had to land on the lake. He began sinking because the seaplane had been holed by the German gunfire, but he was rescued by a Belgian ship. The *Graf von Goetzen* had been put out of action, but more important, the sheer shock of discovering the Allies had aircraft at the lake took all the fight out of the German forces, and they were soon driven from its shores, with the further help of the remaining Short seaplanes. This was one of the earliest examples of the vital importance of air-power in remote wars, and it was achieved with aero-engines and aircraft made in Wolverhampton.

The battle of Kut-el-Almara

A second noteworthy first, achieved by Sunbeam-powered Short seaplanes, was the attempt to supply a besieged garrison by aircraft. General Charles Townshend had been operating with a division in Mesopotamia in 1915, but later in the year superior Turkish forces drove him back into a loop of the Tigris at Kut-el-Almara, where he was besieged for 143 days.

As relief forces were gathered and frantic efforts were made to raise the siege, attempts to supply him by river proved impossible as the Turks held both banks. A supply of grain was discovered within the British Lines, but there was no means of grinding it into flour. Millstones were successfully air-dropped by Sunbeam-powered Short seaplanes.

Following this success valiant attempts were made by RNAS officers to fly in 300 lb bags of flour to the starving troops. The bags, in double sacking, were slung between the floats of the seaplanes, which then had to be manhandled across mud flats, with engines revving desperately, before the flight upstream. The attempts had only limited success, there were insufficient aircraft to ever hope to fully supply Townshend's men, and they were opposed by superior German aircraft flown by the Turks, but they must have delayed Townshend's final surrender for a short while.

It is interesting to note that in the hot and high conditions of Mesopotamia, the two-bladed propellers of the Shorts over-revved the engines, and the local RNAS mechanics, working on two Turkish barges which had been put into use as workshops, fashioned four-bladed propellers from palm-tree wood, a hitherto untried material. The British propellers, in addition, had to be protected in wet sacking because of the heat, something to which the palm-tree wood was better suited!

The Short 184 at Jutland

The most widely produced Short seaplane was the Type 184, and though Sunbeams did not produce any of these themselves, most of the 650 built were powered by Sunbeam

Front fuselage of the Short Type 184 seaplane, No. 8359, in the Fleet Air Arm Museum, displayed in unrestored condition. This was the only aircraft to take part in the Battle of Jutland, powered by a Sunbeam Mohawk, though the engine displayed is a Gurkha, which was fitted after Jutland

engines, 70 with the Mohawk, 53 with a more powerful version of the Mohawk, renamed the Gurkha, and 540 with the later Sunbeam Maori I or II.

The most famous Short 184 of all, serial 8359, was Mohawk-powered and flew at the Battle of Jutland. HMS *Engadine* was ordered by Admiral Beatty to launch a seaplane to search for the German forces. Flt. Lt. F.J. Rutland took off in 8359 with Asst. Paymaster G.S. Trewen as observer and quickly reported the location of the German light cruiser force. The remains of this 184, just the forward fuselage including the engine, is now on display at the Fleet Air Arm Museum, Yeovilton, though the original Mohawk has been replaced with a Sunbeam Gurkha, many of the Type 184s being uprated in this way.

The Short Bomber

The next aircraft actually built by Sunbeam was a batch of fifteen Short landplane bombers, which were powered by the Gurkha. The Short Bomber was heavily based on the Type 184 seaplane, being basically a 184 fuselage with wheels instead of floats and immense wings, the upper ones having an 85 ft span. The prototype, built by Shorts, was powered by the Mohawk, but only the fifteen production aircraft built by Sunbeam itself were fitted with the Gurkha. A total of eighty-three were built by a variety of contractors, all the others powered by Rolls-Royce Eagles.

The Short Bomber had little wartime use before being supplanted by the Handley Page 0/100, but at least one Sunbeam-built version, 9357, attacked the German motor torpedo-boat base at Bruges on 3 February 1917, the only one of three aircraft to reach the target. Because of the advent of the Handley Page, the last five Short Bombers ordered from Sunbeam (9371–5) were cancelled.

Sunbeam Gurkha 255 h.p.

Coatalen increased the power developed by the Mohawk from 225 h.p. to 255 h.p., and the engine was then given a new name. Only eighty-three of this engine were produced, and they were mostly used to replace Mohawks in Short 184 seaplanes.

Sunbeam Zulu 160 h.p.

In the same way the Crusader was enlarged, as with the Gurkha, by increasing the bore from 90 mm to 100 mm to produce the Zulu, which was largely used to replace Crusaders in existing aircraft, only seventy-one being built in all.

Overhead Cam Engines

The side-valve engines, Crusader, Zulu, Mohawk, and Gurkha, suffered from valves that ran very hot, and tended to warp as the engine cooled down after a flight. This was especially so with the Crusader, and mechanics usually removed the engine after every flight for overhaul, and fitted a new one. The Mohawk and Gurkha were hard to start and often needed their plugs heating up before they would fire.

Coatalen had realized that his OHC racing-car engine could provide the basis for a series of aero-engines. He designed a whole range of twin-OHC four-valves per cylinder units, a straight six (Amazon), a V8 (Nubian), two V12s (Cossack and Afridi) and a W18 (Viking), all with cast-iron blocks. They first appeared in 1916, and the V12 Cossack was very widely used.

Sunbeam Cossack 320 h.p.

The Cossack produced 320 h.p. from 18 litres, making it one of the most powerful engines available. It powered the French Bat & Tellier flying boat, which were very successful and served at both Atlantic coast and African bases in some numbers.

The A.D. Type 1000, was a seaplane powered by three Cossacks. This was the largest British aircraft then built, but was restricted to only two prototypes. Most notably the Cossack powered the Short Type 310-A4 seaplane which went into quantity production, a total of 119 being powered by Cossacks.

The Cossack also powered twelve of the Handley Page 0/400 heavy bombers, though six of them were really a half-way house between the 0/100 (one of which had also been powered by a Cossack), with only some of the fuel system modifications that denoted the 0/400. The 0/100 had originally been designed around two Crusaders as the Type 0, but was enlarged when 200 h.p. engines became available. The Sterling Engine Company of Buffalo, New York, arranged to build the Cossack under licence.

Such was the demand for Sunbeam aero-engines and licenced-built aircraft that the company transferred all its car production to an arch rival, the Rover Car Company, in Coventry.

Short 320 seaplane

Sunbeam also built two batches of the Short Type 320 seaplane itself, amounting to forty aircraft in total. These were all fitted with the Cossack engine.

Sunbeam Afridi 225 h.p.

The Sunbeam Afridi was fitted to eighty-five Curtiss R-4 reconnaissance bombers delivered from America with unsatisfactory Curtiss engines, though even with the Afridis fitted they saw little service. The engine also found its way into a number of one-off designs like the Short N.2A Scout. It also powered eighteen Sopwith Type 60 seaplanes and the Wight Type 840 seaplane which went into quantity production, and some of the landplane version. A hundred Afridis were converted to Maoris after manufacture.

Sunbeam Maori 250/275 h.p.

Coatalen developed the V12 Afridi by increasing the bore from 92 mm to 100 mm, the 135 mm stroke remaining the same. It developed 250 h.p. from 12 litres and was called the Maori, over 800 of these being produced. The Maori was probably Coatalen's best large aero-engine and was often fitted to aircraft when the highly successful Rolls-Royce Eagle was not available. Maoris found their way into the Short 184 seaplane, replacing the use of Gurkhas, and 540 were so fitted. Several Fairey seaplanes were also fitted with Maoris, 50 Type IIIAs, 26 Campanias and 54 Type IIIBs.

The Maori was also installed on some Handley Page 0/400s when the preferred Eagles or Liberty engines were in short supply. Continuing the association with Shorts and the RNAS they also powered the Short Type S.419, the last Short seaplane to be built before the Armistice.

Sunbeam Maori V12 OHC 260 h.p. engine on display at the Duxford Aircraft Museum

Sunbeam Manitou 325 h.p.

There was an enlarged version of the Maori with the bore further increased to 110 mm, which gave 325 h.p., but came too late to see active service.

Sunbeam Viking 475 h.p.

Coatalen squeezed an extra bank of cylinders in the Vee of the Cossack to make the eighteen-cylinder Viking, producing 475 h.p. from 27 litres. It had no less than six overhead camshafts, six magnetos and six Wolverhampton-made Claudel-Hobson carburettors. The sheer weight of the Viking seems to have limited its use to torpedo boats, and about fifty-four of these were so fitted.

Sunbeam Nubian 150 h.p.

The 150 h.p. OHC Nubian, none of which was built until 1917, may have been fitted to some of the last of the Coastal class of non-rigid airship. The name Nubian is often quoted as being the Sunbeam engine fitted, but the first Coastal, numbered C1, first flew on 9 June 1915 powered by two 150 h.p. Sunbeams, and must therefore have been fitted with the Crusader. The Nubian was definitely fitted to the twin-engined Blackburn GB.2 seaplane, only two of which were built. Only thirty-six Nubians were built in total.

Sunbeam Arab 200 h.p.

The huge demand for aircraft that built up in 1916 placed tremendous strains on the British aero-engine manufacturers, and the War Office tried to standardize on engines of about 200 h.p. In 1917 Sunbeam had a new V8 engine, called the Arab and it was ordered in large numbers off the drawing board. In January 1917 the Air Ministry had looked at four new 200 h.p. designs, the Arab, the Sunbeam Saracen straight 6, the Hispano-Suiza and the BHP. The Saracen was discounted as being inferior to all the others, 2,000 BHPs were ordered, but it was the untried Arab that received the biggest orders.

It had cast aluminium cylinder-heads and blocks, and developed 208 h.p. from 12.3 litres, and weighed only 550 lb. Over 4,400 of the Arab were ordered not only from Sunbeam, but also under licence from Austin, Lanchester, Napier and Willys-Overland in the USA.

Because of the advanced use of cast aluminium there were inevitable delays and only 81 were delivered before the end of 1917 instead of the scheduled 1,800, and only 1,311 were made before the end of the war. The same problem occurred with the similar Hispano-Suiza V8, built under licence by Wolseley. For a time the War Office had to store engineless SE.5a fighters because of the delays. Most of the Arabs were eventually to be fitted to Bristol Fighters, but some were fitted to Sopwith Cuckoos when their Hispano-Suiza engines were needed for SE.5s.

Despite the high hopes invested in the Arab, which some regard as a copy of the Hispano-Suiza, it acquired a very bad reputation for reliability, and suffered terrible vibration problems. It may have been the last nail in the coffin of Coatalen's reputation.

The Sunbeam Bomber

Like many companies who began licenced-construction of other people's designs, such as Boulton & Paul and Austin Motors, Sunbeam also developed ambitions of producing its own designs. Its only attempt, the Sunbeam Bomber, was so ill-conceived, however, it obviously put an end to any further such ideas.

The Bomber was a single-seat, two-bay biplane of uninspiring proportions. It also suffered from being fitted with Sunbeam's own Arab engine with all its immense teething troubles. The designer obviously wished to place the fuel tank and the external bomb load near to the centre of gravity so that the pilot had to be sited well back in the fuselage. He was fully 9 ft from the single Vickers machine gun on the fore-decking. This was ridiculous in view of the regular stoppages which occurred with the Vickers gun, and the operational need to clear them in flight. Such a remotely-fired gun was a unique feature in a First World War aircraft. The bomb load was normally 3 x 100 lb, but there was provision for more.

An Avro 504K, H2063, in a field behind the orphanage, now the Royal School, Wolverhampton. This was one of the last of the 541 Avro 504s built by Sunbeam probably in 1919 (George Jones)

The first flight of the Sunbeam Bomber was at Castle Bromwich in 1917, and it was still flying at the Air Ministry testing centre at Martlesham in August 1918. It had a span of 42 ft and a length of 31 ft 6 in, weighing 2,952 lb fully loaded. It achieved a top speed of 112 m.p.h. at 6,500 ft, and had a ceiling of 18,500 ft. It was a poorly designed airframe with an unsatisfactory engine, and did not really have a chance of being ordered into production when fine aircraft like the D.H.4 were available.

Avro 504

As well as production of the Short seaplanes, Sunbeam obtained several contracts to build Avro 504 trainers. Firstly they built two batches each of 30 504Bs, and this was followed with 200 No. 504Js and 100 No. 504Ks. A final order for 250 No. 504Ks was amended after the end of the war and only 181 were completed.

Sunbeam Dyak 100 h.p.

A small number of Avro 504Ks were converted by Sunbeams after the war to take their own Dyak engine. This was a straight six with a single OHC, producing 100 h.p. from 8.8 litres. The 504 conversion was fairly straightforward and resulted in a better aircraft than the rotary-powered version. Fuel and oil consumption were greatly reduced, and as the engine could be throttled, unlike a rotary, it was able to tick-over on the ground so that the pilot did not need to switch off. A time between overhaul of 300 hours was achieved by the Dyak, and it was unfortunate for the company that so many dirt cheap rotaries were available at the end of the war, stifling any hope of selling new engines.

A Sunbeam Dyak-powered Avro 504 packed ready for transport, possibly to Dunstall Park. This combination of aircraft and engine performed very well in the Australian bush (George Jones)

In 1920 the Australian Aircraft Corporation built seven 504s powered by the Dyak and these proved very reliable in bush conditions, and more satisfactory than the usual rotary engine. One owned by Arthur Butler, who founded Butler Air Transport, was said by him to be the safest aeroplane he had ever flown. One of these Dyak-powered 504s was the first aircraft operated by Qantas Airlines, and a reproduction of this aircraft has been built with an original Dyak, for Qantas promotional purposes.

The Submarine Scout Twin Type airship, SST13–29 had Dyaks specified, but it was never completed, being cancelled at the end of the war, but some Coastal airships were fitted with Dyaks, and gave good service, both with the RNAS and in Norway and Japan. Other Dyaks were fitted to motor boats and even cars.

Sunbeam Matabele 400 h.p.

Another very large engine designed by Coatalen was the V12 Matabele giving 400 h.p. from 18.2 litres, which was really just a double Amazon, and also limited to motor boat use, though one was experimentally fitted to a DH.4; and of the many engine types fitted to the DH.4 gave performance figures for speed and ceiling second only to the Rolls-Royce Eagle.

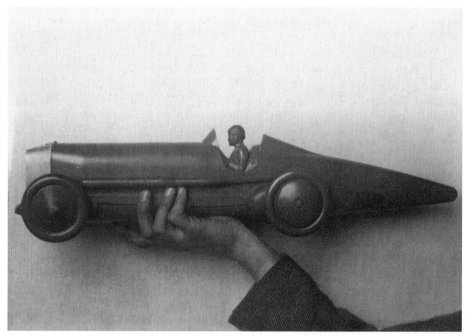

A model of the 350 h.p. Sunbeam, powered by a Sunbeam Matabele engine, presented to Sir Malcolm Campbell after he broke the World Land Speed Record in the car. The model was made by Boulton & Paul in Norwich (they had redesigned the car after tests in their wind tunnel) (Miss L. North)

Sunbeam Sikh 800 h.p.

Before the end of the war Sunbeam had answered a War Office request for a really large engine to power a heavy bomber with a massive 64 litre V12 called the Sikh. It developed 800 h.p., weighed 1,952 lb and had an incredible six valves per cylinder operated by push rods.

The Sunbeam Sikh was also offered for airship use, and a semi-Sikh was developed, a straight-six of 32 litres, which was just one half of the Sikh. Neither of these had significant usage.

The end of the war was disastrous for the aircraft industry. Not only were almost all outstanding orders cancelled, but there was soon a huge stock of war-surplus aircraft and engines to satisfy any demand from military or civil operators. By January 1922 Sunbeam were offering brand new Dyaks from stock for only £295, instead of their normal price of £950, and the V12 Manitou for only £395, instead of £1,250. As late as 1924 the company was taking full page advertisements in *Flight* and the *Aeroplane*, promoting eight different engines, but there were to be no more orders for any of them.

The Sunbeam stand at the 1929 Olympia Aero Show, with the huge 1,000 h.p. Sunbeam Sikh III in the foreground. This was Sunbeam's last fling as an aero-engine manufacturer (George Jones)

The R.33 and R.34 airships

Sunbeam tried to continue engine development against this background of almost no orders. The Maori V12 was installed in the R.33 and R.34 airships, five in each, and Sunbeams also built the propellers. John Marston Ltd of Paul Street, Wolverhampton, supplied the radiators for the engines, and Hobson's the carburettors.

The installation consisted of one engine at the rear of the forward control car, driving a 17 ft propeller, two coupled together in a rear car, driving a single 19 ft 6 in propeller, and one in each of two side gondolas, equipped to operate in reverse, as an aid to ground manoeuvring. The starboard engine had a plate welded to the exhaust pipe, on which saucepans and kettles could be placed. This was the only way of supplying hot food and water to the crew. Any food heated thus had to be carried up an open ladder, in the full blast of the slipstream, into the airship!

It was the R.34 that made the first east–west Atlantic crossing, setting off on 2 July 1919, and arriving in New York on 6 July. The R.34 then returned to complete the first double crossing, setting off on 10 July, and arriving in Pulham, Norfolk on the 13th.

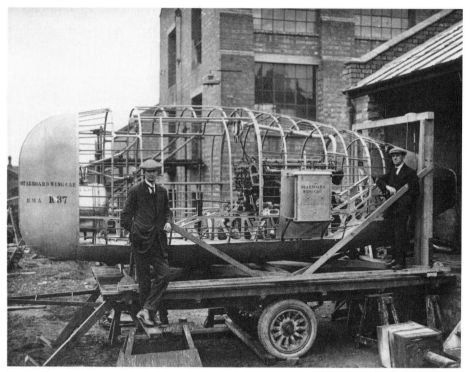

The starboard wing car of the R.37 airship, complete with Cossack engine, ready for delivery from Moorfield Works to Short's at Cardington. The R.37 was scrapped when 90 per cent complete (George Jones)

On the return journey the Maoris gave some trouble, and three had to be shut down before arrival. This was sometimes done anyway, to save fuel, and at least one of the Maoris was not to blame. An engineer fell over and landed on the clutch lever of the starboard engine, so freeing it to exceed its maximum r.p.m. of 2,100, and thus destroying the connecting rods.

On its return to its Scottish base, as a courtesy gesture the R.34 flew over Wolverhampton and circled the Sunbeam and John Marston works.

The R.36 and R.37 airships

Sunbeam provided the engines for the next British airships, the R.36 and R.37. Each was powered by four 350 h.p. Cossacks, and Sunbeam built the entire power gondolas, shipping them to the Inchinnan airship sheds in Scotland and Cardington by truck. Because of stringent economies by the government the R.37 never flew, though it was almost completed, but the R.36 was used for a number of experimental purposes, including – incredibly – traffic control. Using a 675 ft long airship to control the light traffic of the early twenties, seems overkill in the extreme. R.36 was eventually broken up in 1926.

The tragic R.38 airship

The last airship powered by Sunbeam engines, was the R.38. It was begun by Shorts in January 1919, but their airship works at Cardington was nationalized and it was therefore finished by the Royal Airship Works, still at Cardington. It was powered by six 350 h.p. Cossacks. These were much heavier than the engines for which the airship had been stressed, and thus helped lead to its demise.

The airship's first flight was in June 1921, and modifications were required. It was to be sold to the US Navy as the ZR.2. After a girder had broken on its first flight in navy colours, it finally broke in half on 23 August 1921, over the Humber estuary, killing a large number of government airship personnel, many of them being burnt to death by burning petrol on the water.

The Sunbeam Pathan

In 1920 the Sunbeam Car Company joined in a loose amalgamation with Talbot and Darracq, to form S.T.D. Motors. In 1926 Sunbeam developed the Pathan diesel aero-engine. Diesels looked increasingly attractive because of the low fuel consumption and several manufacturers began to develop them. The Pathan was a six-cylinder engine of 8.8 litres which developed 100 h.p. It was based on the wartime Dyak petrol engine, but it did not achieve any success.

Although Sunbeam aero-engines achieved a great deal of success when installed in record-breaking cars, they found little further use in aircraft, though a surprise comeback was attempted at the 1929 Olympia Aero Show. The Pathan and a new diesel version of the Sikh, for airship use, were exhibited. The Sikh III, a 1,000 h.p. V12, was proclaimed to be the world's largest engine, but compared with contemporary engines from Rolls-Royce and Napier, it was, at 2,760 lb, dreadfully overweight, and attracted no interest from the aircraft industry, especially as the crash of the R.101 had put an end to the British Airship Programme.

Louis Coatalen left the company in the twenties and set up his own company in France, to produce diesel aero-engines with French government backing. He spent more and more of his time in France up to his departure, and his going mirrored the decline of a fine company. The Sunbeam car business also finally disappeared in 1935, when the Rootes Brothers acquired the name and used it on Hillman and Humber cars.

Although Sunbeam started the war as perhaps the premier British aero-engine manufacturer, its products were always to suffer in comparison with many of its rivals, especially Rolls-Royce, the other major producer of liquid-cooled engines. Coatalen seemed to produce a large number of different engines, rather than concentrating on fully developing a few designs, and so its engines had a well-established reputation for terrible reliability. Henry Royce in comparison, produced only four engines during the war, the Hawk, the Falcon, the Condor and the marvellous Eagle, which he painstakingly developed from an initial 200 h.p. to 375 h.p. at the end of the war, coupled with marvellous reliability.

Sunbeam seems to have been most highly regarded by the RNAS, and found wide use in a variety of seaplanes. The Mohawk, Cossack, and Maori appear to have been the best engines produced, though there are indications that the Dyak was a very good engine. Perhaps if the Arab had been the success that everyone hoped, instead of one of the worst engines of the war, Sunbeam's reputation might have been held in greater esteem, and it might have survived to become one of the major post-war manufacturers.

13

1915–18, THE ZEPPELIN RAIDS AT PERTON AND KINGSWINFORD

The Zeppelin menace brought a Royal Flying Corps unit to the West Midlands in 1916. No. 38 (Home Defence) Squadron was formed on 14 July 1916, based at Castle Bromwich which had been requisitioned by the War Office at the outbreak of war.

No. 38 Squadron was really reforming and it superseded 54 Squadron, which had moved to London Colney, and included a number of 54 Squadron personnel. It operated detachments at four Staffordshire minor landing grounds, Great Barr, Chasetown, Kingswinford and Perton.

The field used at Perton was not on the site of the later Second World War airfield, but a little further to the west along Perton ridge. It was a 50 acre site called the Fern Fields.

The Kingswinford strip was at Wall Heath. It was behind the Navigation Inn, parallel to the Mile Flat.

No. 38 Squadron used a mixture of BE.2cs, BE.2es and BE.12s, all variations of the same theme. The BE.2 was a pre-war machine designed for the Royal Aircraft Factory at Farnborough by Geoffrey de Havilland. It had a top speed of 72 m.p.h. at 6,500 ft, and was mostly used as an observation aircraft on the Western Front.

The BE.2 had been designed to be inherently stable, something which was seen as important before aerial combat came into existence, when an emphasis on speed and agility was necessary. It could, however, be used against airships, which were even more unmanoeuvrable, and did have successes in the London area. Effective from 1 October 1916, 38 Squadron's were replaced by the more useful FE.2b.

This was also a two-seat biplane, but with a pusher propeller, so that an observer/gunner could sit in the nose in front of the pilot, with a clear field of fire for his one or two Lewis guns. The maximum speed of the later version, with a 160 h.p. Beardmore engine, was 81 m.p.h. at 6,500 ft. A FE.2b was the first aircraft built, under licence, by Boulton & Paul, in their factory in Norwich.

In September 1916 the headquarters of 38 Squadron moved to Melton Mowbray. There were only three Zeppelin raids on the Midlands during the war, but the defenders had no success whatsoever in intercepting them. None of the aircraft that tried to intercept them took off from Perton or Kingswinford.

On the night of 31 January 1916 nine Zeppelins raided the North and Midlands, and most of them became hopelessly lost because of the terrible weather conditions, with fog and freezing rain and snow. Max Dietrich in L.21 dropped 35 fifty kilogram bombs and 20 incendaries on Tipton, in the belief that he was bombing Liverpool. Thirty-three people were killed and twenty injured.

Further bombs fell in the Walsall area, a stick landing down Bradford Street. The mayoress, Mrs S.M. Slater was in a tram outside the Science & Art Institute in Bradford Place, and she died of injuries received when one bomb landed nearby. Further bombs dropped on Birchills and Pleck, and total casualties were four dead and fourteen injured.

A RE.7 of No. 5 Squadron took off from Castle Bromwich, but the pilot never saw the airship. He reported that the centre of Birmingham was completely blacked out, but the suburbs and approach roads were well lit up. On 1 October 1916 eleven Zeppelins raided various targets and some bombs were dropped on Birmingham. A BE.12 of 38 Squadrom took off from Leadenham minor landing ground, but force-landed with engine trouble.

The last raid was not until 12 April 1918. Zeppelin L.62 dropped some bombs south-west of Birmingham and south of Coventry, but they exploded in open country. The FE.2bs of 38 Squadron took off from Stamford and Buckminster minor landing grounds, but both of them crashed in the Coventry area.

One imagines that any personnel detached to Perton and Kingswinford had one of the quietest postings of the whole war, and there could not have been a great deal of flying.

14

1917–19, BOMBER PRODUCTION AND FLYING, SMETHWICK

There was another satellite landing ground in the Black Country, at Halford's Lane, Smethwick, opposite West Bromwich Albion's football ground. This had rather more impressive use than the SLGs at Perton and Kingswinford.

The Birmingham & Midland Carriage Co. built Handley Page 0/400 bombers in Smethwick and these were flown from this specially built airfield, on the west side of Halford's Lane. A total of 104 0/400s were built at Smethwick, and some of these were later to become civil airliners. The 0/400 was a development of the 0/100 twin-engined heavy bomber, fitted with a new fuel system. It only appeared in any numbers towards the end of the war, and only in the last three months were effective bombing raids carried out. The final sixteen of the last batch of fifty ordered were cancelled after hostilities ceased.

The company also built 100 DH.10 Amiens twin-engined bombers, and these were also flown from Smethwick. The DH.10 was a medium bomber, but only eight had been delivered before the end of the war, and only two evaluated on the Western Front. They were powered by two 400 h.p. Liberty engines which gave them a respectable

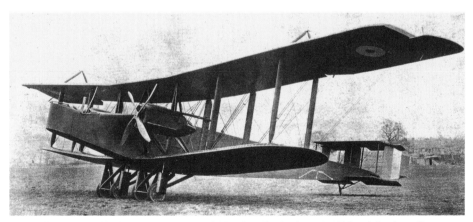

A Handley Page 0/400 heavy bomber as built by the Birmingham & Midland Carriage Co. at Smethwick (D. Jones)

The last DH.10, E6042, a Smethwick-built example, experimentally fitted with twin-rudders at Farnborough (N. Hulse)

performance of 117 m.p.h. at 6,500 ft. After the war they were to pioneer a number of air-mail routes operated by the Royal Air Force, and a few saw service on the North-West frontier. One Smethwick-built example (E6042) served at Farnborough for test purposes, and was fitted with a twin fin and rudder for a while. It continued to fly until 1926 and was the last serviceable DH.10.

Passing down the M5 these days it is certainly hard to imagine an adjacent airfield from which biplane heavy bombers rumbled into the air.

15
1918, AERO-ENGINE PRODUCTION, WOLVERHAMPTON

Guy Motors and Clyno Cars

The War Office engine requirements for the year beginning June 1918 totalled 64,987, and the engine required in the largest numbers (8,580), the ABC Dragonfly, was designed by none other than Granville Bradshaw.

Earlier in the war Bradshaw had built his first radial engine, the two-row, six-cylinder Mosquito, which gave 110 h.p., and did not go beyond the prototype stage. Next was the Wasp, a seven-cylinder radial giving 170 h.p., made in tiny numbers for the BAT Bantam and Baboon fighters, and the Westland Wagtail. One Wasp was built by Guy Motors in Wolverhampton during 1918, but the rest of an order for twelve were cancelled.

ABC Dragonfly engines in production in Clyno Cars' Pelham Street Works, Wolverhampton

The Dragonfly was really a Wasp enlarged from 11 to 23 litres, with nine cylinders. The War Office was very impressed by the fact that Bradshaw demonstrated a power output of 365 h.p. for a weight of only 600 lb, which is why they ordered it in such large numbers. It was commissioned from firms all over the country, including 600 from Guy Motors of Wolverhampton and 500 from Clyno Engineering of Pelham Street, Wolverhampton, but development difficulties limited production when the war ended to only twenty-three engines. A total of 1,147 had been built before contracts were cancelled.

Clyno Engineering made four of its order with another eleven unfinished, when orders were cancelled. Guy Motors was congratulated by William Weir, the Director General of Aircraft Production and Supply, for the speed with which it built its first Dragonfly. A prototype was built in 1918 from first machining operation to initial test-run in the remarkably short time of only twenty-four days, but that was the only one completed before orders were cancelled. At the end of the war Guy was working on its own liquid-cooled V12, but that too was cancelled. Having test-run the Dragonfly Guy Motors had obviously felt it could do much better itself.

The Dragonfly suffered from a number of problems, including high fuel consumption and vibration. Cooling was also inadequate, and the cylinder heads ran a dull red after only a few minutes. A large number of wartime, and post-war aircraft paid the penalty for being designed around the Dragonfly, but Granville undoubtedly was the originator of the high-powered, air-cooled, radial aero-engine, and the government recognized this with an award of £40,000 after the war.

He was to go on to design the ABC Scorpion and Hornet aero-engines and the successful ABC motor-cycles, which were even built by Sopwith Aircraft for a while, when aircraft orders dried up at the end of hostilities.

Star Engineering

In 1918 Star Engineering accepted an order for 400 80 h.p. Renault engines, despite Edward Lisle's pre-war antipathy towards aeronautical production. The 80 h.p. Renault was a development of the earlier 75 h.p. Renault which had seen widespread use in 1914/15. It was a V8 air-cooled engine, with 90 degrees between cylinder banks. It was fitted to DH.6 trainers when the Curtiss OX-5 engine was unavailable. However, only twelve had been completed by Star at the end of hostilities, the remainder being cancelled.

H.M. Hobson

Another Wolverhampton company, H.M. Hobson Ltd, of Cousins Street, built vast numbers of Claudel-Hobson carburettors for aero-engines during the war. Hobson had begun carburettor manufacture for road vehicles in 1911, and quickly turned to producing them for aero-engines once war started. Many Sunbeam engines were equipped with them, including the Cossack, which had four C2S 42s, the Arab with one HC7 and the Maori with four B2S 38s.

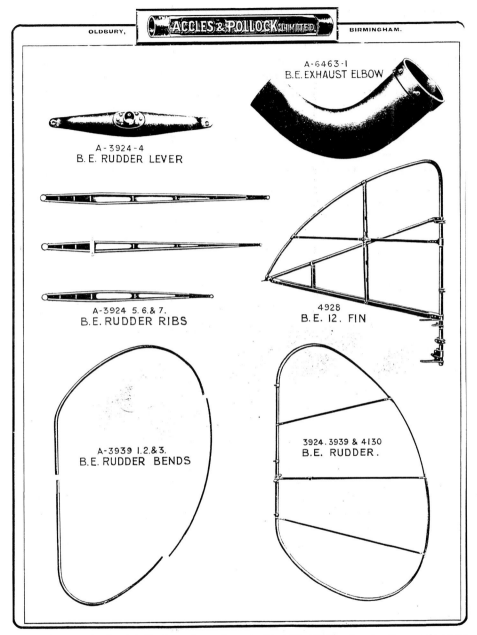

OLDBURY, **ACCLES & POLLOCK** LIMITED BIRMINGHAM.

A-6463-1
B.E. EXHAUST ELBOW

A-3924-4
B. E. RUDDER LEVER

A-3924 5. 6.& 7.
B.E. RUDDER RIBS

4928
B.E. 12. FIN

A-3939 1.2.& 3.
B.E. RUDDER BENDS

3924. 3939 & 4130
B.E. RUDDER.

A page from an Accles & Pollock catalogue from the First World War, showing they made many things aeronautical (Accles & Pollock)

At the Armistice the Black Country had the capability of building complete aircraft. Engines could be provided by four Wolverhampton firms, Sunbeam, Clyno, Star and Guy Motors, with carburettors from Hobson, and radiators for the liquid-cooled engines from John Marston's, also of Wolverhampton. Thompson Bros. of Bilston built undercarriages, tail units and tubular framework, the tubing, of course, coming from Accles & Pollock of Oldbury, who also built such parts as complete rudders, gun mountings and exhaust pipes. Castings, forgings, fasteners, nuts and bolts and even the steel of which they were made came from various firms, and finally aircraft were being assembled by both Sunbeam in Wolverhampton and the Birmingham Carriage Company in Smethwick.

The end of the war and the cancellation of both aircraft and engine contracts had a savage effect on the many companies who had joined in the aviation business. Guy, Star and Clyno went back to road vehicles, and though Sunbeam hoped to continue as one of the country's premier aero-engine manufacturers, it began building its fine cars again, turning back to more peaceful markets.

16

1919–35, PRIVATE FLYING RESUMES IN THE BLACK COUNTRY

The Midland Aero Club did not revive until August 1925 when it became one of five clubs to receive Air Ministry support, with the delivery of its first de Havilland DH.60 Cirrus Moth, G-EBLT, followed by a second, G-EBLW, in September. Flying was at Castle Bromwich however, as there was no airfield in the Black Country.

In 1928 the proprietors of the *Express and Star* donated another DH.60 Moth to the club, and named it *Wulfrun*. Three further Moths were to be bought: two DH.60Xs, G-AABH and G-AADB and a DH.60G, G-AAJJ.

Perton had reverted to agricultural use, but in 1929 permission was granted to V.N. Dickinson of Aero Hire Ltd to operate his Cirrus Moth on instructional flights from there, keeping it in a small shed. He had just competed in the King's Cup Air Race, which was a Round-Britain race in 1929, but retired at Blackpool. In July 1929 the Wolverhampton Light Aeroplane Club was formed with Geoffrey Mander MP as chairman, and they invited Dickinson to move from Castle Bromwich to Perton to undertake instructional flights.

An unusual aircraft, Henderson-Glenny HSF.II Gadfly I, G-AAEY was owned by C.F. Parker of Wolverhampton from May 1931 to February 1933 when E. Bradley of Wolverhampton bought it. It was a single-seat monoplane powered by a 35 h.p. ABC Scorpion designed by none other than Granville Bradshaw. It had been built by Glenny and Henderson of Byfleet and in May 1929 had set a world altitude record in the 200 kg class of 3,021 metres. It was scrapped in June 1934.

From the end of the First World War until the mid-1930s there was very little flying done within the Black Country apart from a handful of barnstormers. Private owners kept their aircraft at Castle Bromwich or on private strips like Perton. One such was Arthur Hill, an ironfounder who lived on the Wergs Road, Wolverhampton, and kept his Gipsy Moth at Castle Bromwich, until he crashed it into a tree near Hinckley in 1933.

17

1920s, Barnstorming round the Black Country

The most notable of the barnstormers were Berkshire Aviation and Capt. Percival Phillips' Cornwall Aviation Company, who toured the country each summer, giving joy-flights at 5s. a time from any town with a field big enough to operate an Avro 504.

As early as 1919 Berkshire Aviation came to Walsall, and gave joy-flights from a field on Calderfields Farm, only a mile from the town centre. It was a very successful

Two Berkshire Aviation Tours' Avro 504Ks flying *very* close together. In September 1924 two of their 504Ks gave 700 people joy-flights at Wolverhampton, while 8,000 people paid sixpence each to come in and watch, and 16,000 more watched from outside the field. Just previously the same two aircraft gave 1,100 people flights in just nine days at Cannock (R.D. Smith)

company, formed by Fred and Jack Holmes, with Alan Cobham as second pilot, and began operating in May 1919 with a base at East Hannay, near Wantage, with assets totalling £900, which consisted of one war-surplus Avro 504K, a Ford car, £50-worth of petrol, and £200 in the bank. In the first year it also visited Wolverhampton, Kidderminster and Shrewsbury. After that first year Alan Cobham left the company but it continued for many years, and operated as many as four 504s. Its success was apparent when the company returned to the same site in Walsall nine years later, and gave over four hundred people a flight, with many more turning up to watch.

Capt. Phillips had won the DFC with the Royal Flying Corps in the Middle East during the war, after which he worked in the family garage. In 1924 he bought G-EBIZ, a war-surplus Avro 504K for £250 and the Cornwall Aviation Company was born. G-EBIZ was to become one of the most famous aircraft in the country, giving the first taste of flying to people the length and breadth of Great Britain, and eventually was converted to take four passengers. By 1929 the fleet had grown to four Avros, often touring the country separately, but sometimes coming together at one venture. By 1931 the company had taken up a total of 95,000 passengers, over 55,000 of them by Phillips himself, with not one injury.

Apart from the aircraft all that was carried in the accompanying truck was a portable wind-sock, and a banner to hang over the gate of the field that would be rented, often for as little as a pound. Publicity would be gained by giving local papers, like the *Express and Star*, tickets for free flights to be won in competitions. Often reporters, always on the lookout for an unusual story, were taken up for free.

People would flock for a flight for 5s., a loop for 10s., or a spin for £1. Many would just come to watch, and the flying was often spiced up with a little wing-walking, or a parachute jump, which was always the highlight, kept to last.

Apart from Calderfields in Walsall, a number of fields spread through the Black Country were also used by the barnstormers. There was a field where First Avenue, Low Hill, is now, in Wolverhampton, and another on the other side of the Wobaston Road from where Wolverhampton Airport was later built. There was another at Mile Flat, Wall Heath, behind the Navigation Inn, the site of the First World War Satellite Landing Ground. There was also an area used for joy-flights on the common at Willenhall. In 1928 and 1929 Capt. Summerfield of the Cornwall Aviation Company gave flights at Blackhalve Lane, Wednesfield, Wolverhampton. He gave three thousand people flights in 1928, but 1929 was not so successful.

18

1929, COBHAM'S AERODROME CAMPAIGN, PERTON

In 1929 Alan Cobham returned to barnstorming with his Municipal Aerodrome Campaign. Through the twenties he had pioneered a number of air routes, and became a household name with such flights as his record-breaking return trip to Australia and a flight to Cape Town. He wanted to make the country more air-minded and for more towns to build their own airports, as had happened in America.

Between May and October 1929 he visited 110 towns and cities throughout the British Isles in a ten-seat, single-engined de Havilland Giant Moth, G-AAEV, which he named *Youth of Britain*. At each location he would meet the local mayor and town clerk, as well as local councillors, and would give them all flights over their home town, and expound on his campaign during lunch. He also gave flights to a large number of local children at the expense of Sir Charles Wakefield, who supported his campaign, and then in the afternoon and evening gave seven-minute flights for the usual fee, which more than covered his costs. During the year he took up 40,000 passengers and made 5,000 landings. Having interested municipalities in having their own airports he then set up as an aviation consultant to advise where to put them.

He began the campaign at Oxford on 25 May and on Saturday, 22 June he arrived in Wolverhampton from Worcester. The *Express and Star* had given him a week's publicity, because he had given it 100 free tickets for use by its readers. He used a field next to Perton Court on the Pattingham Road, and arrived at 11 a.m., being met in the air by the Cirrus Moth *Wulfrun* in which an *Express and Star* photographer was being flown by Fred Sutcliffe.

He gave flights to the mayors and officials from not only Wolverhampton, but also Walsall, Wednesbury and Stourbridge. He then gave the free flights to fifty Wolverhampton schoolchildren, before retiring to lunch at the Victoria Hotel, and a reception given by the Mayor of Wolverhampton. After his usual speech in favour of municipal airports he returned to Perton to give joy-flights at 10s. a time. There were several hundred people present on Saturday, but that was nothing compared to the following day's attendance.

There were special buses laid on, but people flocked there in cars and on foot. A traffic jam clogged the lanes for miles around, and keeping order on the field itself was almost impossible. The crowds would close around the aircraft after each landing, and on one occasion as Cobham was taking a quick meal in the cockpit he shouted for them to keep back, spraying crumbs over them!

Alan Cobham's DH.61 Giant Moth, *Youth of Britain*, G-AAEV (N. Hulse)

There was up to a two-hour wait for flights, which in the morning were largely over Penn Fields, and in the afternoon, largely over Tettenhall. Each flight lasted 5 minutes with 3 minutes allowed to change the ten passengers. People who had flown before in open-cockpit barnstormer's aircraft marvelled at the comfort of the enclosed cabin, and one of the lucky winners of the *Express and Star* free flights, expressed the opinion that he felt perfectly safe, because it was 'A British-built aircraft'! Perhaps overlooking the fact that one of the big stories of the week was the crash of a British-built Imperial Airways airliner into the Channel. The traffic jam away from Perton was even more horrendous than the one in the morning, and from the air looked like several stationary giant black snakes.

An incredible picture of Martin Hearn on the top wing of a Cornwall Aviation Co. Avro 504K with Cobham's National Aviation Days. Unlike modern 'wing-walkers' who are securely strapped to a frame, Hearn is only holding on with a rope tied to the top wing, and the aircraft is flying over the crowd, which would never be allowed today (R.D. Smith)

19

1930s, Cobham's Flying Circus Round the Black Country

Cobham's famous name drew the people to Perton, but by the early thirties the days of the one-aircraft barnstormer were numbered and Cobham put together a Flying Circus in association with the Cornwall Aviation Company, and began touring the country from the spring of 1932. Cobham was still anxious to improve the air-mindedness of the British people and he therefore named the shows the National Aviation Day Displays.

For four years shows were put on almost every day throughout the summer months, moving from town to town. On 9 May 1932 the Flying Circus was at Calderfields, Walsall, the only visit to the Black Country that year. The following year it returned again, having split at the beginning of June into two separate tours. The number two tour came to Walsall on 1 June, and the number one tour came to Kitchen Lane, Wednesfield, Wolverhampton on 30 July. The displays were a huge success, and required an organization that ran like clockwork.

Kitchen Lane and Calderfields were typical venues. The ground staff would arrive first, usually very late at night from the previous venue. Early in the morning they would put a 6 ft fence round the field to stop people watching the show without paying their 1s. 3d. entrance fee. The field would already have been tested for its suitability by running a car over it at 60 m.p.h. Next, trees in the way of take-offs and landings were often cut down, and the spectator enclosure was made ready, usually with the sun behind it, if at all possible. Farmers were remunerated, and were usually happy to have their fields used. Air Ministry approval for each field had to be obtained beforehand, and there was a whole department just satisfying this requirement for the barnstormers.

One team had the responsibility of putting up signs all over the locality saying 'To the Air Display', and then taking them down again in the evening.

The display was preceded by a formation flight in which all the aircraft taking part were filled with paying customers. The display consisted of aerobatics, air-races, novelty items, such as flour-bombing and crazy-flying. There were both male and female parachutists, and a display of aerobatics by a BAC.VII two-seat glider. One pilot, in a Tiger Moth, would snatch a handkerchief off the ground with a hook on his wing-tip; A wing-walker named Martin Hearn climbed all over an Avro 504K in flight, and ended up sitting on the skid while it was looped. Such unattached wing-walking was banned in June 1933, and 'wing-walkers' these days have to be securely strapped to a harness in a standing position.

Joy-flights went on during the display with a constant stream of aircraft taking people up on what was often their first flight. These ranged from a fairly sedate flight around the town in a small airliner, such as one of the two Airspeed Ferrys, which Cobham had commissioned for just this venture, named *Youth of Britain II* and *III*, or an even larger Handley Page Clive (G-ABYX) with twenty-two seats. Those brave enough could be taken for a loop in a two-seat biplane for a £1. A quick circuit in a ten-seat Ferry was 10s., and throughout the display pilots would be taking up passengers, four at a time in 504Ks, on a seven minute circuit for as little as 4s.

There was soon a rival, the British Hospitals Air Pageant, begun in 1933 by Charles Scott, who with Campbell-Black was to win the 1934 England to Australia Air Race. Some of the proceeds went to local hospitals wherever they performed. Captain Phillips was attracted by these aims and transferred his allegiance, his fleet of 504Ks, as well as his new Spartan three-seater. It only lasted one season, however, but it performed in 185 towns, including Stafford where they flew from the Common. Miss Staffordshire, Mabel Thurstone of Penkridge, was given a free flight by Charles Scott himself.

There was intense rivalry with Cobham all summer, but it was Scott who came off worst, barely covering his costs. After the Hospitals Air Pageant folded Captain Phillips returned to Cobham for the 1934 season, but gave up the Spartan, which he did not like, for a Mongoose-powered Avro 504.

Rotary wing flight was so unusual it was an obvious attraction for Cobham to use in his Circus. This is one of two Cierva C.19 Mk.IVPs used by Cobham, G-ABUF (R.D. Smith)

The amount of organization required for Cobham's tours, and the amount of work put in can be illustrated by three days of the 1934 tour. On 14 July there was a show in Bristol, the following day it was once more at Kitchen Lane, Wednesfield, and on the 16th it was at Aberystwyth, and there were no motorways for the convoy of vehicles to use. On 8 June the show had once more been at Walsall, but the following year Walsall was a late stop on the tour on 20 September.

In 1935 there were again two separate tours, the *Astra* tour, lead by the Handley Page Clive named *Astra*, and the Ferry tour, led by a new Airspeed Ferry. They included for the first time a Cierva C.19 autogyro, which amazed the crowds, few of whom had seen a rotary wing aircraft before.

For the first time Dudley was included on the itinerary with a two-day display on 21 and 22 April by the *Astra* tour. The field used was actually at Mile Flat, Wall Heath, a long-standing barnstormer's venue, and on 21 April, which was Easter Sunday, there was a crowd estimated to be 20,000, but the following day the weather was bad and numbers were down. Cobham had followed his usual policy and gave the *Dudley Herald* thirty vouchers for free flights to give to its readers, thereby gaining valuable free publicity. Joan Meakin, who did a display of aerobatics in a Wasp glider, entertained the crowd by broadcasting by radio, over the loudspeakers, as she went through her routine. Naomi Heron-Maxwell and Ivor Price, the two parachutists were pulled simultaneously off the opposite wings of the Handley Page Clive, by their parachutes.

Joan Meakin, the 'Glider Girl', who was usually towed aloft by an Avro 504 (R.D. Smith)

Cobham's Handley Page Clive, G-ABYX,with a parachutist just being pulled from his seat on the lower port wing, by deploying the parachute while still on the wing (R.D. Smith)

The *Astra* tour called twice at Wolverhampton during 1935. On 6 June they made their usual stop at Kitchen Lane, Wednesfield, and on 22 September they came to Perton, showing the fact that it was in use for flying, as it was described in the advertisement as 'Perton Aerodrome'.

Cobham was becoming a victim of his own success. In making the country air-minded, he was removing the mystique of flying, and people were no longer willing to pay to see anything so commonplace. Whereas the *Express and Star* carried a report of the 1933 display, highlighting the upside-down flying of Turner Hughes in his yellow Tiger Moth, and the crazy-flying of Jock Mackay, who pretended to be a drunken spectator hijacking an Avro, the 1934 and 1935 displays did not even rate a mention.

At the end of the 1935 season Cobham sold most of the aircraft to Charles Scott and Captain Phillips, who toured in 1936 under the name British Empire Air Displays, later changed to C.W.S. Scott's Flying For All Air Displays. They visited 150 towns, including Wolverhampton, where the venue was once more Kitchen Lane, Wednesfield on 16 August. The wind was strong enough on the day of the display for R.J. Astley to be able to fly his autogyro backwards! Throughout the year the weather was bad, and the day of the Flying Circus was over. In September the official receiver was appointed.

Cobham and the other barnstormers had given tens of thousands of people their first chance to fly. From the first tour of the Berkshire Aviation Company in 1919, for a mere 5s., people could in perfect safety do what men had only dreamed of doing only twenty years before, what no Englishman had done until only ten years before.

20

1935, FLYING FLEAS IN WOLVERHAMPTON AND WALSALL

In the mid-thirties Flea-fever hit Great Britain. A Frenchman, Henri Mignet, designed a tiny single-seat, tandem-winged aircraft, which he called the Pou-de-Ciel, or Sky Louse. He claimed that anyone who could build a packing case could make one and teach himself to fly. The first British-built one, dubbed Flying Flea, first flew in 1935, and soon amateur and professionally-built ones were appearing all over the country.

There was such interest in the Flea that Cobham had included one in his final tour, and even used it on his advertisements. When the tour came to Cosford on 6 September, flying from a field on the other side of the A41 from the later airfield, a

Three Henri Mignet HM.14 Flying Fleas in various stages of construction

report of its attempts to fly merited the sole mention of the display in the *Express and Star*. On its first attempt the little engine would not start, but after being pushed to a distant part of the field to be worked on, a second attempt was slightly more successful. The pilot managed to coax it into the air, but the engine coughed loudly just over the first hedge and the Flea landed three fields away.

The following year Charles Scott included a Flea in his display, but as an advertising gimmick, showing it at Vauxhall car dealerships, like Attwoods in Wolverhampton, in the week before a visit by his Flying Display.

One Flying Flea, G-AEME, was built in Wolverhampton by R. and D. Weaver. It was first registered on 26 August 1936. Three Birmingham-built Fleas were tested at Walsall Airport, G-AEBT, G-AEFI and G-AEOH. Construction of another Flea was commenced at Walsall Airport. A club member, Harry Griffiths, and the ground engineer, Jock Ogilvie, were partners in the venture, but the first part of this Flea to be built, the rudder, was actually constructed by young Eric Holden.

Unfortunately the Flea was an inherently dangerous device, and several of them killed their pilots. This resulted in the Flea being banned, after eighty-three had received Permits to Fly, and many more had been started but not finished. G-AEME's registration was cancelled in December 1937, and the Griffiths/Ogilvie Flea at Walsall remained unfinished.

However, legitimate aircraft production was about to return to the Black Country. In 1935 Boulton & Paul's aviation division in Norwich was closed, and a new public company was formed, Boulton Paul Aircraft Ltd, and this was based in Wolverhampton, the move being complete by August 1936. The council, as one of its means of attracting the new company had agreed to give Boulton Paul flying rights at the brand-new Wolverhampton Airport, for a hundred years.

As soon as the factory was finished, its first product, the Hawker Demon two-seat fighter, began to be flown from the airfield, as well as other aircraft for test purposes. Though Boulton Paul was the first occupant of Pendeford Airport, private flying was soon to follow as Wolverhampton opened its first civil airport since Dunstall Park had faded away before the First World War.

21
1935, THE OPENING OF WALSALL AIRPORT

Alan Cobham promoted air-mindedness, and encouraged towns to open municipal airports, but he garnered a certain amount of financial reward from this by often acting as a consultant in choosing airport sites, many of which were later to prove ill-advised.

In 1929 Cobham came to Walsall and toured the town with the Borough Surveyor. He recommended the Aldridge Lodge Estate, between Longwood Lane and Bosty Lane, for use as an airport, despite the fact that it was on a hillside. Walsall Council purchased the estate and some surrounding land to a total of 220 acres, but it was not until June 1933 that work began on preparing it for use as an airport.

Surrounding trees were cut down, as well as some of the larger hedges, and a small hangar was erected next to a clubhouse, situated near the upper end of the airfield, to give a good view. The hangar cost £1,460, and the clubhouse £1,250.

On 1 June 1933 Cobham's National Aviation Day Display again came to Calderfields, though Cobham himself was not present. The Mayor of Walsall announced that discussions were going on with surrounding councils such as Sutton Coldfield, Wolverhampton and Birmingham, with a view to co-operating in setting up a West Midlands regional airport, but civic pride prevented these discussions going very far.

The Walsall Aero Club was formed by a number of interested local people to fly from the new airport, and their first aircraft was a second-hand Miles Hawk monoplane, G-ACRB, which cost £425. This was the aircraft with which Fred Miles had really launched himself as a light aircraft manufacturer, based on the purchase of a batch of cheap Cirrus engines released from an abortive sale to Canada, which allowed him to undercut the price of all rivals. Bill Holmes was engaged as flying instructor at the princely sum of £250 per annum, plus 5s. an hour flying pay.

The club struggled to survive on the limited flying being done. The running of it was taken over for a while by two men named Bayley and Bilson who brought a Hermes-powered Desoutter, G-ABMW, high wing monoplane to the airport. To raise money the Hawk was replaced by an older Avro Avian biplane, G-AAVM. In October 1934 Bayley and Bilson left, followed by the instructor, and the club was on the verge of closing down.

A crisis committee of club members was formed to try and retrieve the situation, and the club was reformed with a new name. The South Staffordshire Flying Club was created in June 1935 to operate the airport. About fifty of the Walsall Aero Club members joined the new club, for whom J.H.A. Wells became the chief flying instructor, and Jock Ogilvie the engineer. A lady named Mrs Gabrielle Patterson also

became an instructor, apparently the only female flying instructor in the country. The
Avro Avian, G-AAVM was its sole initial equipment.

The club was launched and the airport officially opened with an air display on 4 July
1935, and among the aircraft participating were a de Havilland Dragon, G-ACON, of
Crilly Airways, a BAC Drone, a Miles Falcon, a Blackburn Bluebird, G-EBRF, a
Westland Widgeon III, G-EBRN, a Junkers monoplane, G-EBZV, and a Puss Moth,
G-ABCR.

With the opening of the airport, Helliwells Ltd, a Dudley engineering company,
decided to expand there, and construction of a factory began on the Walsall Road site.
They went on to build Wellington bomb beams.

The South Staffordshire Flying Club added a second Avian, G-ABCD, to the
fleet, then in May 1938 a Gipsy Moth II was purchased, followed in June 1938 by a
Tiger Moth, G-AFGW. The Avian G-ABCD crashed at Perry Barr on 8 March
1938.

Private owners also kept their aircraft at Walsall, including a Widgeon, G-EBRO,
owned by a Mr Ivor Tidman and Bert Yardley, a Puss Moth, G-ABIU, owned by Mr
E. Baker, and a Gipsy Moth, G-AAHY, owned by Mr Hill of H. & J. Hill, of
Willenhall, which was later replaced by a Hornet Moth. Harry Griffiths was another

Ivor Tidman's Westland Widgeon, G-EBRO, a Walsall Airport resident before the war
(Eric Holden)

club member with his own aircraft, a Comper Swift single-seater powered by a little Pobjoy engine.

Harry Griffiths was present when a Tipsy two-seat monoplane, G-AESU, was demonstrated in 1936. This little aircraft, powered by a 62 h.p. Mikron engine was designed by E.O. Tips, the manager of Fairey Aviation's Belgian factory, and with a few modifications it was offered for sale in this country. The demonstration pilot, Mr E. Ward, offered to let Mrs Patterson take it for a flight, but when she refused, Harry Griffiths volunteered. He taxied down to the canal end of the field and took off towards the trees by Aldridge Lodge. For some reason he did not seem to gain much height and appeared to make a 90° turn to the left, and then a 180° diving turn to the right over the trees, crashing into them. The crash removed the engine and fuel tank but Harry walked away with only a bleeding nose.

Needless to say Harry Griffiths did not buy a Tipsy, but he was more attracted by a demonstration of the Klemm Swallow, a low-wing, tandem-seat two-seater. The demonstration claimed that it was impossible to stall, in fact if you could stall it, he said you could have it for nothing! Harry bought a Swallow.

On 23 April 1936 there was a very unusual visitor to Walsall Airport, a Vought Corsair, flown by Flt. Lt. Edwin Shipley, a founder member of both the Walsall Aero Club and the South Staffordshire Aero Club. This American single-engined bomber monoplane had been purchased by the Air Ministry to examine the modern techniques of all-metal stressed skin construction used in America. Shipley flew it up from Martlesham Heath to Castle Bromwich, and made a brief stop at Walsall.

On 2 July 1938 Amy Johnson arrived for a sail-planing display arranged jointly by the South Staffordshire Flying Club and the Midland Gliding Club, who had a field at Handsworth. Six thousand people turned up to watch her fly, and she was towed into the air, slipping the tow at about 2,000 ft. After two successful flights in which she performed loops and side slips, on her third flight, as she was coming in to land the Kirby Kite, she was caught in a down draught and a wing-tip hit a hedge. The glider turned over and she was found hanging in her straps. She was taken away to hospital but was not badly injured.

In November 1938 a Handley Page Harrow twin-engined bomber tried to land at Walsall Airport, but as the longest runway was only 950 yards, and the grass was wet, it ran out of room and skidded through the hedge at the bottom corner between Longwood Lane and the Walsall Road, and came to rest on the main road. The pilot gave his reason for trying to land as engine trouble, but rumour had it that he was only stopping to visit his girlfriend, who lived in Walsall!

One of the maintenance staff at Walsall was Eric Holden, who started as a young man. He had to pay a substantial fee to be taken on as an apprentice, which was the normal system in those days. He later went on to work for the Midland Aero Club at Castle Bromwich. He learned to fly at Walsall, having his first lesson on 13 April 1939 and his first solo on 4 May. After working at the Castle Bromwich shadow factory during the war, and coming back to Walsall to work for Helliwells, he later became Manager of Wolverhampton Airport.

The legendary Amy Johnson with her Kirby Kite glider in which she gave a demonstration of aerobatics on 2 July 1938 at Walsall Airport. The South Staffs. Flying Club's Miles Hawk, G-ACRN is in the background (Eric Holden)

The South Staffordshire Flying Club's Avro Avian, G-ACRN, being worked on by Eric Holden outside the hangar (Eric Holden)

Utility Airways' Fox Moth, G-ACEY, after its crash at Walsall Airport (Eric Holden)

The club held a garden party on 24 September 1938, with a limited display of light aircraft. Unfortunately one of the participants crashed. A Fox Moth G-ACEY, of Utility Airways, flown by Fl. Lt. W. Hill was taking off uphill, with no wind, and with four passengers in the little cabin. He realized that he could not make the aircraft climb, and deliberately switched the engine off and stalled into the trees just beyond the airfield. Luckily no one received anything more than minor injuries.

22

1936, THE OPENING OF
WOLVERHAMPTON AIRPORT

Only one week after the Mayor of Walsall had announced that discussions were going on with other local councils about sharing an airport, Wolverhampton's General Purposes Committee proposed the reservation of 132 acres at Barnhurst Farm for use as Wolverhampton's municipal airport. The question had been raised some years earlier but nothing had been done, until about a year before when Cobham had been asked to choose the best of twenty-five sites in the locality. Despite a large body of opinion that

The Mayor of Wolverhampton, Councillor R.E. Probert, looking suitably aeronautical beside the Midland Aero Club's first Tiger Moth, G-AEOE, at Pendeford Airport (Eric Holden)

felt Perton was an infinitely better site, one he had twice used himself, he chose Pendeford.

Geoffrey Mander, MP, was a keen supporter of the proposal, but one councillor proposed the postponement of the airport project, with the view that building a Civic Centre was more important. The Sewerage Committee could not release the land for two years, and so nothing could be done until 1935.

Work on Wolverhampton Airport cost £127,000, including the building of a single hangar and a small terminal/clubhouse. Flying at Wolverhampton Airport began shortly after 1935, especially by Boulton Paul who made the move from Norwich during late July/early August 1936, but the airport did not open officially until 27 June 1938 with an air display organized by the Midland Aero Club.

The Midland Aero Club would now operate from both airfields, though it would shortly move from Castle Bromwich to the new Birmingham Airport at Elmdon. It was to run Pendeford on behalf of the Council. The earlier Moths had all been sold and replaced by five de Havilland Moth Majors. Another Moth Major, G-ACOH, had been lost in a collision with a Hawker Hart in 1934. The club also had one Tiger Moth, G-AEOE. All club aircraft would operate from both Wolverhampton and Castle Bromwich/Elmdon as demand dictated.

Aircraft gathered for the official opening of Wolverhampton Airport on 25 June 1938. Behind the Miles Falcon Six, G-ADLC (which won the 1935 Kings Cup Air Race), is Amy Johnson's Kirby Kite, a Monospar, G-ACHU, and a Miles Hawk Trainer. Behind those are five RAF Gloster Gauntlet's and a Fairey Battle – the RAF's very latest bomber (Eric Holden)

Chief flying instructor was Wilfred Sutcliffe, who had previously been in the RFC and RAF. In 1939 he was to become chief test pilot of Rolls-Royce. In addition there were two other instructors, Mitchell and Verney-Cave, to share the work load.

The instructors took part in a number of events in the Opening Day Flying Display including balloon-bursting and car-bombing competitions. The Royal Air Force displayed a number of their new aircraft including Fairey Battle, Armstrong-Whitworth Whitley, and Bristol Blenheim bombers and aerobatics by a Gloster Gauntlet fighter, and a Hawker Hind trainer.

The Avro test pilot, S.A. Thorn, gave an aerobatic display in an Avro Tutor, and there were two parachute descents from club Moths, by Mr A.G. Hill and Miss Ray Clark. Miss Clark only narrowly avoided landing in the canal, a built-in hazard on two sides of Pendeford.

The legendary Amy Johnson, obviously fully recovered from her crash at Walsall, was towed to 2,000 ft in a Kirby Kite glider and went through an aerobatic routine on her descent.

Finally there was to be an RAF set piece display reminiscent of those at Hendon, though not quite on such a spectacular scale. A mock house on the airfield was to be 'attacked' by a squadron of Hawker Hind light bombers, and 'defended' by the 209 Anti-Aircraft Battery, a Wolverhampton TA unit. It turned out to be rather less well planned than Hendon, and proved a rather humorous end to the afternoon's events.

The Avro Type 626 Tutor, G-ACFW, outside the single hangar. It was demonstrated in the display by Avro's Test Pilot, S.A. Thorn (Eric Holden)

Amy Johnson and Flying Officer A.E. Clouston (second right) outside the new clubhouse at Pendeford on the official opening day (Eric Holden)

To start with, 209 Battery, obviously full of enthusiasm in front of their home town, opened fire well before even the air-raid siren went, without a bomber to be seen. After the guns fell silent the Hinds attacked, and two apparently 'crashed in flames' without a shot being fired, to the laughter of the crowd. The other three Hinds then circled the airfield for half an hour, with the AA gun barrels following them round. The announcer said there had been a misunderstanding and asked the crowd to imagine that the planes were attacking so that the show could go on!

Mock mustard gas bombs exploded and the ARP wardens, who had been patrolling impatiently, went to work rescuing 'casualties'. The Hinds were then supposed to return to drop high-explosive 'bombs', but they continued to cruise serenely round! Wilfred Sutcliffe and another instructor saw the problem, rushed to two of the club's Moth Majors, and took off to take the place of the Hinds. Obviously it wasn't their fault that the 'bombs' exploded before the Moths flew over the target, and it wasn't the firemen's fault that the petrol-soaked house was set alight before they were ready, and was completely burnt out before a hose was directed at it! The Hawker Hinds eventually left, and the crowd went home having thoroughly enjoyed a spectacle worthy of Charlie Chaplin himself.

Later in the year the *Express and Star* presented another aircraft to the Midland Aero Club, the Foster-Wikner Wicko, G-AFJB. At Eastleigh, Messrs Wikner and Foster designed a strut-braced, high-wing monoplane to try and compete on price and performance with the contemporary Miles Hawk. It was built of wood for simplicity, and when it first flew in 1936 had a 90 h.p. Ford V8 car engine, which cost only £60 plus the reduction gear necessary to reduce r.p.m. from 3,300 to 1,500. As it only had a single ignition system it did not receive a Certificate of Airworthiness, and the Ford was replaced with an inverted Cirrus Minor.

N.B. Graham, joint proprietor of the *Express and Star*, saw the Wicko demonstrated at Birmingham Airport, and bought it the same day. It was named *Wulfrun II* and presented to the Midland Aero Club for use in training pilots in the Civil Air Guard scheme. In return the Midland Aero Club agreed to train four pilots nominated by the paper, free of charge each year. The Civil Air Guard had been instituted that year to train pilots at subsidized rates, provided they agreed to join an appropriate service in times of war. Both the South Staffordshire Club at Walsall and the Midland Aero Club were among sixty that rushed to join the scheme.

The Wicko was not entirely suitable for the scheme, it was rather crudely made. Wilfred Sutcliffe's view of it was that the best thing to do with it was 'Take out the engine and set a match to the rest of it.' The Wicko was requisitioned at the start of the war, renamed Warferry, serial DR613, and used as an air taxi by the Air Transport Auxiliary, which ferried military aircraft. Making nonsense of Sutcliffe's lack of faith in it, the Wicko still survives to this day, preserved by a private owner, at his house in Coventry.

One of the club's Moth Majors, with Mitchell instructing, hit a main power cable, and crashed. Wolverhampton was blacked-out for a while, but Mitchell and his pupil both walked away from the crash, if not the embarrassment. The Moth Majors were replaced by six more Tiger Moths, all delivered in February 1939, and registered sequentially G-AFNP/R/S/T/U/V.

The Tiger Moth was to be the most familiar sight at Wolverhampton Airport for the rest of its existence, but the cosy nature of club flying was shortly to be replaced by the rigours of military training. The Tigers were bought by Shackleton Aviation, acting as consultants for the Royal Air Force, and Tiger Moths were shortly to return to Pendeford in military colours.

23

1936, BOULTON PAUL AIRCRAFT LTD COMES TO WOLVERHAMPTON

Boulton & Paul Ltd was a structural engineering and woodworking company in Norwich, and like many such firms was brought into aircraft manufacture during the First World War. Its first aircraft was an FE.2b, which flew in 1915. It built 225 FE.2bs altogether, followed by 300 FE.2ds, 1,575 Sopwith Camels and 425 Sopwith Snipes. It also built the wooden hulls of 70 F.3 and F.5 flying boats.

Like many such subcontractors, Boulton & Paul soon developed ambitions of building its own designs. The company built extensive experimental research facilities, including even a wind tunnel, and as head of this new department John D. North was recruited from Austin Motors in Birmingham. He had been Production Superintendent at Austins, laying down production lines for R.E.7 and R.E.8 aircraft built under licence; despite the fact that he was only twenty-three.

Before the war North had been Chief Designer at the Grahame-White Aircraft Company, which he had joined in 1912. Not getting on with Herbert Austin, North was happy to move to Norwich and set up Boulton & Paul's experimental aircraft department.

The company's first design, for a fighter to replace the Sopwith Camel, was the P.3 Bobolink, but the rival Sopwith Snipe was chosen for the contract. There followed the P.6 experimental light aircraft and then the outstanding P.7 Bourges, a twin-engined bomber with fighter-like manoeuvrability and performance, which came just too late to pick up any orders.

In the '20s and early '30s Boulton & Paul struggled to survive on a trickle of contracts for prototype aircraft and subcontracts for other companies. Some rivals like Martinsydes went out of existence, others, like Glosters, were swallowed up by the more successful firms.

Boulton & Paul managed to survive, and despite its history as joinery manufacturers, became a pioneer in the use of steel-strip in aircraft construction. It was for this reason that it made the structure of the R.101 airship, and John North was responsible for all detail design. A steel-strip structure featured in the company's first significant aircraft design to go into production, the Sidestrand bomber.

The twin-engined Sidestrand first flew in 1926, and drew immediate praise for its manoeuvrability, continuing the tradition of the earlier P.7 Bourges. It was able to loop, spin and roll, and had a top speed of 140 m.p.h. Only eighteen were ordered to equip one squadron, No. 101, and they entered service in 1929, but even such a small order was a godsend in lean times.

Boulton Paul's new Flight Shed, with an Overstrand bomber, K8175, to give the picture scale. This aircraft was engaged on various turret trials, and is shown without a nose turret fitted (John A. Chambers)

The high speed of the Sidestrand convinced North that the nose gunner deserved some protection from the elements, and so he designed a fully-enclosed, power-operated turret for installation in a new version of the Sidestrand. The circular turret, containing a single Lewis gun was powered by compressed air in bottles topped-up by a compressor attached to one of the aircraft's Pegasus engines.

The resulting Overstrand was the first aircraft in the world to have such a turret. Three more Sidestrands were converted and a new production run of twenty-four Overstrands was begun in 1934, again only equipping 101 Squadron.

The Overstrand was the last of the company's designs to be built in Norwich, and the last of its biplanes. In 1934 the aircraft division of Boulton & Paul was sold off, and became Boulton Paul Aircraft Ltd. A new era was dawning and the company was moved to Wolverhampton.

A French engineer, De Boysson of the Société d'Applications des Machines Motrices, had developed a four-gun electro-hydraulic turret, but the French government was not interested. John North, with his work on the Overstrand, saw the potential of the turret and bought the rights. The electro-hydraulic system was superior to his own compressed-air system, and this decision was to form the basis for the whole future of the company.

The first aircraft to be manufactured at the new Wolverhampton factory was another biplane, the Hawker Demon two-seat fighter. In 1931 the high performance of the Hawker Hart single-engine bomber, which exceeded that of contemporary RAF fighters, led to the development of a fighter version, which was eventually called the Demon.

The first of 106 Boulton Paul-built Demons flew on 21 August 1936. When fitted with a Mark V Kestrel engine of 584 h.p. the Demon was capable of 182 m.p.h. at 16,400 ft, and it was felt that the gunner needed some sort of protection from the slipstream. From October all Boulton Paul Demons were fitted with a Frazer-Nash hydraulic turret, with a folding shield, which had been tried out on the original J9933. The development was known as the Turret-Demon. Production of the Demon was completed in December 1937.

The expansion of the new factory was rapid, most of the eight hundred workforce from Norwich had made the move, but further skilled labour had to be recruited in Ulster and Scotland, and a training school was also set up in Cannock. The main factory was eventually extended to cover over three times its original area, besides subsidiary factories and stores. It seems that the men who came from Norwich did not get on with the local men initially, thinking they had to come to teach the natives a bit about engineering. The local recruits, who had just come from the newly closed Sunbeam Car Company in many cases, did not take kindly to the notion that Black Country men needed to be taught anything about engineering. Things were made worse by the fact that the Norwich men held most of the senior posts. However, the animosity soon disappeared and they all began to work together quite happily.

One Norfolk man, who had been happy in the rural surroundings of Norwich, wondered what on earth he had let his family in for, as their train rolled through the black, smoky towns of Tipton and Bilston. In those days men had to move to where the work was, but he was more than gratified when he found the new factory was set in beautiful countryside on the other side of Wolverhampton, well away from the smoke and the grime.

The Defiant

The most famous product of the company was under construction even before it left Norwich. In the late thirties there was much argument over the best armament for the modern fighter, and the advent of the power-turret introduced a new element. Many looked back on the great success of the two-seat Bristol Fighter of the First World War, and felt a turret-equipped monoplane would be the modern equivalent. In any case, the RAF needed a replacement for the Hawker Demon, which new monoplanes were already making obsolescent, and the Air Ministry issued Specification F.9/35, which called for a two-seat fighter with the main armament concentrated in a power-operated turret.

It was also required that the new fighter would have a performance approaching that of the latest single-seat fighters, with manoeuvrability to match. The three main contenders emerged in 1935 as the Hawker Hotspur, the Bristol 147 and the Boulton Paul P.82 Defiant. The Defiant was the aircraft chosen for production.

It was similar in size and shape to the Hurricane, but because of the turret weighed about 1,500 lb more. In order to balance the extra weight, to achieve the required performance, the Defiant had a smaller wing-span and less wing area than the Hurricane.

The Defiant was Boulton Paul's first all-metal, stressed-skin aircraft. Great lengths were gone to to try and counter the drag of the turret. A very smooth surface was obtained by rivetting the skin while flat, and using counter-sunk holes. In front and behind the turret were wooden fairings, which rose when the guns were in the fore and aft position – for aerodynamic cleanliness – but which hydraulic cams depressed automatically to allow the guns to traverse. The aircraft was powered by a Rolls-Royce Merlin I of 1,030 h.p.

Construction of the prototype, serial K8310, had begun in Norwich, but continued through 1936 at Wolverhampton, and the first flight, at Pendeford, was on 11 August 1937, at the hands of Flt. Lt. Cecil Feather, Boulton Paul's chief pilot. To begin with, it flew without the turret, but with ballast carried to compensate.

Flight trials continued into 1938, and revealed the need for slightly larger vertical tail surfaces, and these were incorporated into the second prototype that first flew on 18 May 1939, powered by a Merlin II. A tailwheel replaced the skid of the first prototype. The Defiant proved to be an excellent flying machine with few vices.

The first production order had been placed even before the Defiant had flown, for they were perilous times, eighty-seven Defiants being ordered in March 1937. The first production aircraft with a Merlin III flew on 30 July 1939, and was delivered for trials at the Aeroplane and Armament Experimental Establishment in September.

The prototype Defiant, K8310, before the turret was fitted, on the taxiway from the factory to the airfield (Dowty Boulton Paul Ltd)

The prototype Defiant, K8310, now with its turret fitted (Dowty Boulton Paul Ltd)

It had a speed of 303 m.p.h. at 16,500 ft, and a loaded weight of 8,350 lb. The turret fitted was the Boulton Paul 'A' Mk.IID with four Browning .303 machine guns, and provision for 600 rounds per gun.

The Blackburn Roc

The Royal Navy had also seen a need for a turret-equipped fighter and issued Specification 0/30/35. The contract was won by the Blackburn Roc, which was basically a Blackburn Skua dive-bomber fitted with a Boulton Paul Type A four-gun turret. A navalized version of the Defiant had been offered by Boulton Paul, but its high landing speed probably mitigated against it. Blackburn was too busy with production of the Skua and the Botha light bomber, and so the order for 136 aircraft was subcontracted to Boulton Paul, who did all the redesign work on the Skua. The first three production aircraft (L3057–3059) served as prototypes. The first Roc was flown by the Blackburn test pilot on its initial flight at Pendeford on 23 December 1938, but Cecil Feather did all subsequent testing.

The prototype Blackburn Roc, L3057, just before its first flight at Pendeford on 23 December 1938. Boulton Paul built all 136 Rocs, and redesigned the Blackburn Skua to take the Boulton Paul four-gun turret (Boulton Paul Society)

Production Rocs outside the factory, which is apparently being camouflaged by one poor man with a brush. He is on the smallest of his three ladders, obviously taking a rest from climbing the long one! His work was all in vain because during the war Lord Haw Haw announced that Boulton Paul had camouflaged the factory, but had forgotten the little white house on the hill

The Roc was never a success, though it was embarked on carriers for a short while and operated for a few months from shore stations. Its 890 h.p. Bristol Perseus gave it a top speed of only 223 m.p.h. at 10,000 ft, slower than any bomber it might have met. Its stablemate, the Skua, proved a better fighter if anything. At least it had forward firing guns, so that it did not actually have to overtake its prey before firing.

John North falls on his head

John North was working on another turret-equipped fighter, besides the Defiant. On 26 May 1937 the Air Ministry issued Specification F.11/37 for a two-seat day and night fighter for Home Defence. The gunner was to be in a power-operated turret equipped with four 20 mm Hispano cannon, which either would be able to fire forward, or there would be supplementary fixed forward firing guns. It was to be capable of at least 370 m.p.h. at 35,000 ft.

Six companies tendered for this aircraft, and the Boulton Paul project, designated P.92, was chosen. A contract was placed in March 1938 for three prototypes. To test the aerodynamics of their design, Boulton Paul had Heston Aircraft build a half-scale wooden replica, the P.92/2, with a fixed undercarriage and powered by two D.H. 130 h.p. Gipsy Major engines. After only three hours flying the P.92/2 showed that the aerodynamic layout was totally satisfactory, and had good handling characteristics.

A mock-up of the P.92 was constructed, which included a working example of a revolutionary escape system for the pilot. Because the propeller blades were so close together just behind the cockpit, the pilot's seat was arranged to tip back, so that in an emergency he could slide out of the bottom of the aircraft upside-down. John North tested this system himself, with a net rigged beneath the mock-up to catch him. Unfortunately the net was not taut enough and North banged his head on the floor. After three days off work North summoned the technician responsible for the test to his office. The poor wretch headed for the great man's office, fearful of the worst as John North did not have a reputation for treating fools kindly. After a few moments North looked up from his desk. 'Well, it worked didn't it?' was all he said.

The company did a great deal of development work on the P.92, but on 26 May 1940 the project was cancelled, when construction of the first prototypes was 5 per cent complete. The Air Ministry had decided to concentrate on the production and development of existing types. The requirement was filled largely by the Bristol Beaufighter.

The Defiant goes into service

With re-armament and re-equipment of the Royal Air Force in full swing, further production orders for the Defiant were issued making a total of 363 Defiants at the outbreak of the war. A further order for 150 was placed in December 1939 and 50 more in February 1940.

One Defiant, L6950, was equipped with bomb racks in August 1939 to test the type's suitability for ground attack operations. In many ways the Defiant was an ideal ground attack aircraft. It was rock-solid in a dive, and a wonderful front-gun platform (if only it had been fitted with front guns).

Comparative trials were undertaken by 111 Squadron in October 1940, between the Defiant and the Hurricane I. The report indicated that with its huge disadvantage in wing-loading and power-to-weight ratio, the Defiant would not have a chance against any competent Hurricane pilot. This certainly did not bode well for the future.

The first squadron deliveries were made in December 1939 to 264 (Madras Presidency) Squadron at Martlesham. In late February the squadron undertook dive-bombing trials at Orfordness and finally became operational on 20 March 1940. The following day they were posted to Wittering, followed by a move to Duxford on 10 May. The first action occurred on 12 May. 'A' Flight with six Defiants flew a patrol along the Dutch coast with Spitfire top-cover. They saw bomb splashes around a destroyer and shot down a Junkers Ju.88.

The following day 'B' Flight flew a similar patrol with orders to strafe German troops. They encountered some Junkers Ju.87s and claimed four shot down. Then they were attacked by Messerschmitt Bf.109s and were hopelessly outclassed. In a desperate battle five Defiants were shot down, for the loss of only one Bf.109.

The Defiant's finest hour

Subsequent operations over the Channel resulted in claims by 264 Squadron for sixty-five kills by the end of May, fifty-seven of them during the last five days of the month, including an amazing total of thirty-seven during only two patrols of twelve aircraft on the 29th.

It has been shown from *Luftwaffe* records that these claims were greatly exaggerated, only fourteen German aircraft were lost in all actions on 29 May, but there is no doubt that this was the Defiant's finest hour. A large part of its success can be explained by the German pilots mistaking the Defiants for Hurricanes, and attacking from the rear, only to suffer a rude shock when coming under fire from forty-eight machine guns. They were not to make the same mistake again; seven Defiants were shot down on the 31st.

These events over the Dunkirk beaches were to cause the Air Ministry to place a further order in July for 280 aircraft, but 264 Squadron had been forced to withdraw to lick its wounds and to train replacements.

On 4 June 1940 Winston Churchill was to express the officially held satisfaction with the Defiant at that time, when he said in the House of Commons, 'All our types, the Hurricane, the Spitfire, and the new Defiant, and all our pilots, have been vindicated as superior to what they have at present to face.' This was an unfortunate choice of words in the case of the Defiant, whose pilots were very anxious not to be in the position of 'facing' a Bf.109, or indeed almost anything else, as a head-on-attack would render them helpless!

The King at Boulton Paul

In April 1940 King George VI and Queen Elizabeth visited Boulton Paul Aircraft. They saw an aerobatic display by a Defiant on the airfield and then toured the factory. In the drawing office they spoke to five of the girl tracers, the ones nearest the door, and then they waved goodbye to the rest, causing many of them to break into tears of disappointment. The royal party then inspected the Defiant production lines and the new aircraft standing on the apron.

In response to RAF requests Boulton Paul had fitted two Mark I Defiants with Merlin XX engines giving 1,260 h.p. At the same time changes were made to the cowling and radiator, and a pressurized fuel system adopted, together with extra fuel tankage. With these changes the aircraft was designated Defiant Mark II, and had a top speed of 313 m.p.h. at 19,000 ft.

The last order for 280 aircraft was amended to 63 Mark Is and 210 Mark IIs, and the last seven Mark Is were changed to Mark II standard on the production line. Delivery began in January 1941 and ended in February 1942.

The original prototype, K8310, was rebuilt during 1940 as a mock-up of a single-seat fighter with four forward-firing guns, but this scheme was not proceeded with. A pre-war scheme for a dual-control trainer was never built.

The second Defiant Squadron was No. 141, which received its first aircraft on 4 April, and was declared operational with fourteen Defiants on strength on 3 June, based in Scotland. It moved to West Malling in July. In their first action nine Defiants were scrambled to meet a mixed force of Ju.87s and Bf.109s off Dover. The Defiants were attacked from directly astern, a blind spot for the gunners and six were shot down, though 141 Squadron claimed four Bf.109s.

This combat proved conclusively that the Defiant was no match for a Bf.109 and they were withdrawn to Prestwick where they would only encounter bombers. No. 264 Squadron had little more success in daylight operations. The basic problem was the lack of forward-firing guns. The pilots had to work out complicated three-dimensional geometry in their heads in order to place their aircraft in a position where the gunner could fire. The Bristol Fighters in the First World War had been flown as single-seat scouts, because they had forward-firing guns, with the extra dimension of a gunner to protect their tail. The Defiant pilots could not do this.

The switch to night-fighting

It was decided to transfer both squadrons to night-time operations, where, before the advent of airborne radar, they at least had the advantage of two pairs of eyes. In some ways the turret was also an advantage at night. A fixed-gun fighter had to open fire when the target was silhouetted against the darkest part of the sky, the horizon. A Defiant could open fire from beneath, with the target silhouetted against the stars.

Further squadrons were slowly equipped with soot-black Defiants to operate against the German night raiders. No. 96 Squadron was the third to fly Defiants, followed by 255, 151, 256, and 307. In addition 85 Squadron had used them alongside Hurricanes for a while.

Two Operational Training Units used Defiants, No. 54 at Church Fenton and No. 60 at Leconfield, but both also had Blenheims. Eventually the Defiants were concentrated at Leconfield and the Blenheims at Church Fenton.

The Defiant had moderate success as a night fighter, and some were to be fitted with Airborne Interception radar sets, operated by the pilot. This was of dubious value as the cathode tube ruined the pilot's night vision, and distracted him from his instruments at the same time. Priority for the best A.I. equipment was given to the twin-engined Blenheims, and later Beaufighters. They had the advantage that their pilot's head could remain up, night-vision unimpaired, while their navigators studied the radar screens.

Other squadrons that operated the Defiant in the night-fighter role were 125, 153, 409, 410, and 456, as well as 515 (Special Duties) Squadron. As Defiants were

The Boulton Paul test pilots in front of a Defiant night fighter. Left to right: chief test pilot
Fl. Lt. Cecil Feather, George Skelton, and Robin Lindsay Neale (later to lose his life in a Balliol
crash) (Dowty Boulton Paul Ltd)

replaced by twin-engined aircraft they were released for whatever roles could be found
for them. In February 1942 tests were undertaken to study their suitability for air-sea
rescue work, to replace Lysanders in the role.

Rescue equipment was redesigned to fit their wings, and two sets of dinghies
were carried in bomb containers. The Defiant seemed suitable and began to equip
281 Squadron in March. Fifty Defiants were converted in all, and were used by
four other Air Sea Rescue Squadrons. In operational use there was to be a change
of heart, and the smaller turning circle and lower speed of the Lysander were seen
to have been an advantage. Defiants were phased out of this role from November
1942.

A few Defiants were equipped with electronic jamming equipment and operated
over the Channel in 1942 jamming German radar as an aid to Bomber Command. They
were thus the world's first 'Wild Weasel' aircraft, until supplanted by bigger aircraft as
more and more electronic equipment had to be carried.

A radar-equipped Defiant night-fighter on display in St Peter's Gardens, Wolverhampton, between the fountain and the art gallery

The Defiant target tugs

Another new role for the Defiant was to be as a target tug, its most important of the war. Such extensive modifications had to be made to suit it for this role that a new set of Mark numbers were given.

The T.T.Mk.1 was based on the Mark II with the Merlin XX engine. The turret was removed and replaced by the drogue box beneath the fuselage and a winch within the fuselage. An enclosed observer's position was provided, and the all-up weight was much the same as the fighter version, but the extra drag reduced the top speed to 250 m.p.h.

A production order for 140 was placed in July 1941, and the prototype T.T.Mk.I was delivered from Pendeford on 31 January 1942. With no new fighter versions needed, the last forty Mark IIs were built as T.T.Mk.Is as well. Some earlier Mark IIs were also modified.

The T.T.Mark II was fitted with the Merlin 24 giving 1,620 h.p., and much work was done to reduce the loaded weight to 7,500 lb. The T.T.Mark III was the Mark I fighter converted to a target tug, and the conversion of 150 was commenced in January 1942. Some of them were fitted with tropical filters in a chin location.

The use of Defiant target tugs was very widespread, for anti-aircraft batteries, and

A Defiant T.T.I. target tug, DR972, at Pendeford (Boulton Paul Society)

air-to-air use for both fighters and bombers. They were to find their way as far afield as Cyprus, South Africa and India, as well as all over the United Kingdom. More than one Defiant was transferred to the Indian Air Force.

During 1943 about sixty Defiant target tugs were transferred to the Royal Navy, who also used them in this country and abroad. They served in North Africa, the Gold Coast, Trinidad and Ceylon, among other locations. A few Defiant tugs were even transferred to the USAF.

One Defiant, DR925, found an historic role of its own. It was transferred on 11 December 1944 to Martin-Baker Aircraft for their first airborne ejection seat trials. A few other Defiants were used in experimental work, at Farnborough and elsewhere, but the type was finally declared obsolete in July 1945.

The last Defiant had been completed in February 1943, and a total of 1,062 had been built. The Defiant was born of an ill-conceived concept, and suffered accordingly. It was designed as a bomber destroyer at a time when no one gave a thought to the possibility that attacking bombers might be escorted by single-seat fighters, and that German fighters would be operating from the coastal airfields of France.

The Defiant did what it was designed to do, but a fighter without forward-firing armament was soon found to be a misnomer. As an interim night-fighter it achieved a great deal of success, and as a target tug it did important but unglamorous work. The Defiant played its part, and is rightly remembered as the best-known product of Boulton Paul Aircraft.

It is a shame that only one remains, N1671, a Mark I which saw service with 307 (Polish) Squadron and ended its career as a target tug. Having managed to survive the scrapman's attention it has had its turret returned and has been repainted in night-fighter camouflage in the colours of 307 Squadron, and is displayed in the Battle of Britain Museum in Hendon.

John North was offered one at the end of the war, as a mark of thanks for the company's war effort, but he had obviously had enough of turret fighters, because he turned the offer down.

Wartime gun turrets

Boulton Paul's engineering staff had been given over entirely to the development of aircraft armament, while the factory produced both complete aircraft and gun turrets. Further production of Boulton Paul turrets was also licensed to Joseph Lucas Ltd and other companies.

As early as 1938 an order was received for a power turret for the Lockheed Hudson. Further turrets followed with both machine guns and 20 mm cannon. Dorsal turrets were fitted to the Lockheed Ventura and Martin Baltimore; dorsal and tail turrets to the Consolidated Liberator; and the full set of nose, dorsal and tail turrets to the Handley Page Halifax. The Halifax tail turret was unusual in that the ammunition for the four .303 guns was carried within the aircraft's fuselage and fed into the turret through its base.

The Boulton Paul P.105 naval multi-role aircraft in reconnaissance form, with rear armament (Boulton Paul Society)

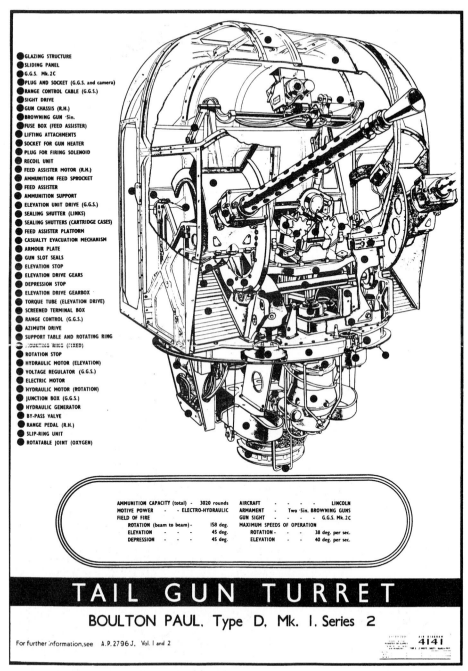

GLAZING STRUCTURE
SLIDING PANEL
G.G.S. Mk.2C
PLUG AND SOCKET (G.G.S. and camera)
RANGE CONTROL CABLE (G.G.S.)
SIGHT DRIVE
GUN CHASSIS (R.H.)
BROWNING GUN ·5in.
FUSE BOX (FEED ASSISTER)
LIFTING ATTACHMENTS
SOCKET FOR GUN HEATER
PLUG FOR FIRING SOLENOID
RECOIL UNIT
FEED ASSISTER MOTOR (R.H.)
AMMUNITION FEED SPROCKET
FEED ASSISTER
AMMUNITION SUPPORT
ELEVATION UNIT DRIVE (G.G.S.)
SEALING SHUTTER (LINKS)
SEALING SHUTTERS (CARTRIDGE CASES)
FEED ASSISTER PLATFORM
CASUALTY EVACUATION MECHANISM
ARMOUR PLATE
GUN SLOT SEALS
ELEVATION STOP
ELEVATION DRIVE GEARS
DEPRESSION STOP
ELEVATION DRIVE GEARBOX
TORQUE TUBE (ELEVATION DRIVE)
SCREENED TERMINAL BOX
RANGE CONTROL (G.G.S.)
AZIMUTH DRIVE
SUPPORT TABLE AND ROTATING RING
MOUNTING RING (FIXED)
ROTATION STOP
HYDRAULIC MOTOR (ELEVATION)
VOLTAGE REGULATOR (G.G.S.)
ELECTRIC MOTOR
HYDRAULIC MOTOR (ROTATION)
JUNCTION BOX (G.G.S.)
HYDRAULIC GENERATOR
BY-PASS VALVE
RANGE PEDAL (R.H.)
SLIP-RING UNIT
ROTATABLE JOINT (OXYGEN)

AMMUNITION CAPACITY (total) - 3020 rounds   AIRCRAFT - - - - LINCOLN
MOTIVE POWER - - ELECTRO-HYDRAULIC   ARMAMENT - Two ·5in. BROWNING GUNS
FIELD OF FIRE   GUN SIGHT - - - - G.G.S. Mk.2C
   ROTATION (beam to beam) - 158 deg.   MAXIMUM SPEEDS OF OPERATION
   ELEVATION - - - 45 deg.   ROTATION - - - 38 deg. per sec.
   DEPRESSION - - - 45 deg.   ELEVATION - - 40 deg. per sec.

TAIL GUN TURRET
BOULTON PAUL, Type D, Mk. I. Series 2

For further information, see A.P.2796J, Vol. I and 2

The Boulton Paul Type D Mk.1 Series 2 tail turret with twin 0.5 inch machine guns for installation on the Halifax and Lincoln

The Fairey Barracuda

When Defiant production came to an end it was replaced in the factory by licensed production of the Fairey Barracuda. This was a result of Specification S.24/37, issued in November 1937, for a naval dive-bomber/torpedo/reconnaissance aircraft. Fairey won the contract in January 1940.

The Barracuda was an unusual-looking, high-wing monoplane with a high set tail. Its sheer ugliness was due to the varied roles the designers had had to try to incorporate. The high wing was to give the crew downward visibility for the reconnaissance role, and this meant an immensely long and strong undercarriage was needed, made even longer by the fact that room for a torpedo under the fuselage was also required. One of the more repeatable nicknames bestowed upon it was 'the pregnant stork'. The wing was so high that special handles had to be fitted near the tips because deck crew could not reach them to manoeuvre the Barracuda on the ground. An American naval pilot, seeing a Barracuda for the first time, expressed the opinion that the Fleet Air Arm would do better if they were equipped with aeroplanes.

The Mark I was powered by a Rolls-Royce Merlin 30 giving 1,300 h.p., which was not enough for such a large aircraft, and only thirty were manufactured by Fairey. The

The Fairey Barracuda production line at Pendeford on 10 July 1942 (Dowty Boulton Paul Ltd)

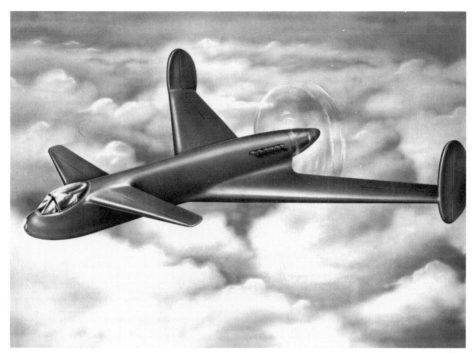

An artist's impression of the Boulton Paul P.100 low-level attack fighter. This aircraft was never built (Boulton Paul Society)

Mark II was fitted with a Merlin 32 of 1,640 h.p., and orders were placed beginning in 1941 for 1,688 aircraft, with licensed production by Boulton Paul for 300.

The Barracuda saw widespread service with the Royal Navy. Its most famous action was the first carrier-launched dive-bombing attack on the German battleship *Tirpitz*, in a Norwegian fiord. The ship was severely crippled from fifteen hits from 500 and 1,000 lb bombs. Two more attacks on the *Tirpitz* were unsuccessful.

The Barracuda Mark III was an anti-submarine reconnaissance version with an ASV Mk.X scanner in a radome under the rear fuselage. The prototype was converted from DP855, which was the first Boulton Paul-built Barracuda. Production orders for 600 Mark IIIs were received by Boulton Paul, of which 392 were built. The last 208 were cancelled at the end of the war. Suddenly, once more, peace had descended with a shock, which was to quieten many factories.

24

1939–45, WOLVERHAMPTON AIRPORT AT WAR

In 1941 Air Schools Ltd, who operated No. 16 Elementary Flying Training School at Burnaston near Derby, was asked to open another at Wolverhampton Airport, to try to cope with the heavy demand for pilots. The new school, designated No. 28 EFTS, officially opened on 1 September 1941, under the control of No. 51 Group, Flying Training Command.

Air Schools Ltd had been formed in 1938 to operate a Reserve Flying School at Burnaston equipped with Hawker Hinds. In the same year the company opened Derby Aero Club, and then at the outbreak of war it set up No. 16 EFTS, operating up to 108 Miles Magisters.

The first course of thirty pupils arrived at Wolverhampton on 11 September and there were thirty Tiger Moths resident initially, though this number was to rise steadily. When No. 17 EFTS closed at Peterborough in May 1942, that unit's thirty-six Tiger Moths were brought to Wolverhampton, which by now had reached its assigned strength of 108, divided into six equal flights.

To accommodate this mass of aircraft the original solitary hangar had been augmented by three more standard 'T' Type hangars, and a large hutted camp was created behind them.

The operation of so many trainers, none of which had radio, must have been a nightmare, especially as Boulton Paul-built aircraft were using the airfield as well. All that station operations had, to prevent trainee pilots landing on top of one another, was a Very pistol, as a last minute warning. It is a tribute to the organization at Pendeford that there were no collisions.

This did not prevent crashes taking place elsewhere. One Tiger Moth had engine trouble over the Bushbury area and the instructor tried to land it in front of the Britool works. Both he and his pupil did not survive the resulting crash. At least two other Tigers crashed on the Marsh Lane playing fields, on the approaches to the airfield.

As well as aircraft built by Boulton Paul being tested from Pendeford, aircraft that were fitted with Boulton Paul turrets often used the airfield in connection with the installations. Early in the war Lockheed Hudsons were often to be seen, and later on a Halifax flew in, though taking off again from such a small field was a marginal operation, involving putting the Boulton Paul tail turret as near as possible to the fence at the canal end and hoping the bomber was airborne before Marsh Lane was reached!

To ease congestion a Relief Landing Ground at Penkridge was established for

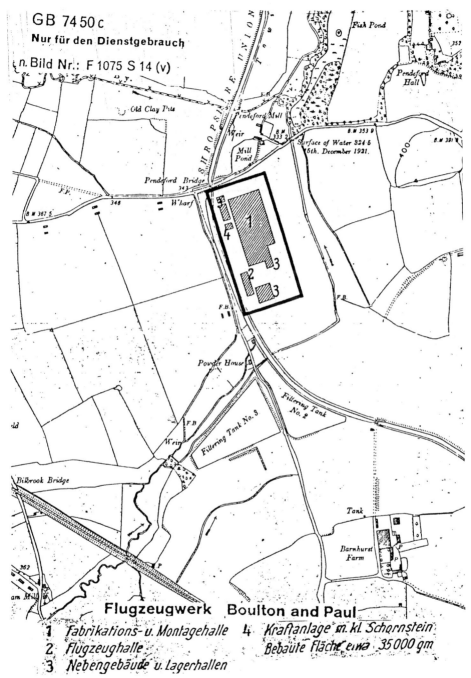

GB 74 50 c

Nur für den Dienstgebrauch

n. Bild Nr.: F 1075 S 14 (v)

Flugzeugwerk Boulton and Paul

1 *Fabrikations- u. Montagehalle*   4 *Kraftanlage m. kl. Schornstein*
2 *Flugzeughalle*   *Bebaute Fläche etwa 35 000 qm*
3 *Nebengebäude u. Lagerhallen*

A *Luftwaffe* bombing map of Boulton Paul. *Luftwaffe* aerial photographs showed both the real and dummy factories, so they were not fooled, but the sole bombing attack hit the sewage works

No. 28 EFTS, where most of the night-flying training was undertaken, away from the industrial smog of Wolverhampton, and the balloon barrage. Burnaston's RLG at Battlestead Hill, near Burton-upon-Trent was also used for a while. Amazingly, considering the RLGs were equipped with hangars and other huts, the Tiger Moths all came in to Wolverhampton for lunch. The circuit at such times must have looked like a host of Moths round a flame!

The airfield and the Boulton Paul works both featured on German target maps, but only one raid was recorded against the factory. At around 6.45 p.m. on Sunday, 29 September 1940 a lone Junkers Ju.88 emerged from cloud to the west diving over the factory and then swung back. It ignored the dummy factory, which had been set up further along the canal towards Brewood, and turned back towards the well-camouflaged real thing, disregarding the mock-anti-aircraft guns on top of the hill. It dropped four or five bombs that missed the factory and exploded in the Barnhurst sewage beds.

On a quiet Sunday evening the pom-pom gunners on Boulton Paul's roof must have been half asleep, because they did not open fire until the bombs had exploded, and the bomber was flying away over Bushbury. The Ju.88 was hit, however, and might have been the one that crashed that evening in the Nuneaton area.

In 1942 secret negotiations were undertaken with Turkey to try and prevent her coming into the war on Germany's side, and Winston Churchill personally intervened. Part of the deal struck with the Turks was that the RAF should train some of their pilots, and Wolverhampton hosted the elementary part of their training. By the end of the war the EFTS was used mainly for refresher training and for training pilots of other foreign air forces.

In 1947 No. 28 EFTS became No. 25 Reserve Flying School, to provide refresher training for pilots on the Reserve List. Air Schools Ltd operated it, but the pilots and staff were now on civilian contracts. The aircraft used were twelve Tiger Moths, but the following year it was decided to give refresher flying to navigators and wireless operators 'as well, thus two Avro Ansons Mark 1s were added, later to be replaced by Mark 21s. The Tiger Moths were replaced by de Havilland Chipmunks, but not for long.

In 1953 there was a review of pilot training, and it was decided that it was unprofitable to train National Service recruits as pilots for only a two-year stint, and all training was to be concentrated at RAF airfields. The Reserve Flying Schools were to be closed, and the first to go on 31 March was No. 25 at Wolverhampton. Reserve officers finished their stint on the reserve with flying at Castle Bromwich.

25
1939–45, WALSALL AIRPORT AT WAR

Walsall Airport was also commissioned by the military during the war, but Helliwells were responsible for most of the flying. They became the 'Mother' company for the North American Harvard trainer. They were responsible for uncrating and assembling them, and later for modification work and repairs. Peter Clifford was their chief test pilot for this work. An experimental hangar was built alongside their main hangar, where Wellington bomb beams were being built at the rate of eight per week. A Hurricane repair contract was also carried out, and this was followed by another 'Mother' contract for Douglas Boston/Havoc light bombers.

Operating Havocs out of such a tiny, sloping grass airfield, even though it was extended as far as it could be towards Bosty Lane, must have taken a degree of steel nerve, and quite a few drops of sweat. A Blenheim trying to land during the war did exactly what the Harrow did before the war, and went right through the hedge onto the main road, where it unfortunately hit a passing truck, killing the driver. This is why test flying, and final adjustments on the Havocs were done at RAF Perton. Only someone desperately rushing out with a Very pistol to warn him away stopped a B-17 Flying Fortress from trying to emulate the Blenheim!

No. 43 Gliding School was based at Walsall, and gave flying experience to ATC cadets from all over the West Midlands. The school operated six Kirby Kites and Kirby Kadets, which were towed into the air by winch. Courses were run that lasted from six to eight weeks.

Further courses were organized for experienced pilots converting to gliders, and coming from the gliding school at Burnaston, Derby. The gliding school finally closed down in 1947 and, like Pendeford, the airport returned to purely civil flying.

26
1941–6, RAF PERTON, WOLVERHAMPTON

Construction of RAF Perton, on the northern edge of Wolverhampton, began soon after the war started. At the peak of the construction effort seventy-three vehicles were hauling ash from Lower Gornal and stone from Oldbury. It was designed and built as a fighter station, echoing Perton's use in the First World War.

It had earth-banked dispersal revetments, and three runways laid out in the usual RAF triangular pattern, two of 1,100 yards, and one of 1,400. A single type T.2 hangar was built on the northern side of the airfield.

Plans for its use changed, and when it was officially opened on 28 August 1941, it was assigned to 70 Group Army Co-operation Command. However, there was no flying for several months.

The headquarters building, RAF Perton, now incorporated into Wrottesley Park House, an old people's home, next to the traffic lights on the A41 (Royal Netherlands Princess Irene Brigade)

Queen Wilhelmina of the Netherlands inspecting the Princess Irene Brigade at RAF Perton in August 1941 (Royal Netherlands Princess Irene Brigade)

In the autumn of 1941 the Princess Irene Brigade of the Dutch Army moved into the accommodation units. On their first day they occupied ten huts and found to their dismay that the water had not been connected. They had to take their water from a bowser parked on the road. Members of the Dutch royal family, including Queen Wilhelmina were to visit the camp, which also included the nearby Wrottesley Hall.

The soldiers developed a good relationship with the local community and several of them married local girls and stayed in the area after the war. A plaque in nearby Codsall Church acknowledges the hospitality enjoyed by the Dutch soldiers and the links forged.

On 27 September 1941 No. 764 Defence Squadron moved from Firbeck to guard the airfield, but the first aircraft did not land until 11 November. A Miles Magister trainer, serial N7626, made a forced landing. Unfortunately for the pilot work on the runways had not quite finished and he hit a pile of rubble, damaging the aircraft; an inauspicious start to flying operations.

In December the Parachute Training School at Ringway was looking for a new base away from built-up areas, both for secrecy and presumably to avoid trainee parachutists descending in droves onto people's houses. As Perton was vacant they inspected it, but decided it was also too near built-up areas.

In January 1942 No. 11 Service Training School at RAF Shawbury, north of Shrewsbury, had a training backlog because the grass airfield had been waterlogged and runways were being built. On 19 January Perton was transferred to No. 21 Group Flying Training Command, to become a relief landing ground for Shawbury. A flight of fourteen Airspeed Oxfords was moved in on 21 January, Perton's first flying unit.

The Oxford was to be the aircraft most associated with Perton. It was a military development of the small Envoy airliner which first flew in 1934; a low-wing monoplane with two Armstrong-Siddeley Cheetah engines. There were 400 in service at the outbreak of war and 8,757 were built in all, numerically one of the most significant wartime aircraft. The Oxford was mostly used as a multi-engine and crew trainer, and had a maximum speed of 182 m.p.h. at 8,300 ft.

Runway construction having been completed at Shawbury, the Oxfords were able to return there in March. On 7 May, 764 Defence Squadron also left, for Snailwell, and the defence of Perton was assumed by No. 4035 Special Flight of the RAF Regiment.

On 1 June the station was made a satellite of RAF Tern Hill, an airfield also suffering both from waterlogging, and overcrowding. Flights were detached to airfields all over Shropshire and on 14 June five Miles Masters arrived at Perton. They were part of No. 5 (Pilots) Advanced Flying Unit, and flying began immediately with a regular programme of advanced flying training, including cross-country flights. This was the most usual role for the Master, of which 3,300 were built during the war. Master Is were powered by 870 h.p. Rolls-Royce Kestrels, and Master IIs by Pratt and Whitney Twin Wasp radials of 825 h.p.

It was a Master II that was involved in the only serious crash at Perton. The Wasp engine of one of three aircraft taking off towards the Dutch Camp blew a cylinder. The trainer lost height and crashed into a ploughed field just beyond the camp. When the fire-crew arrived they found it standing on its nose. The pilot, who was unhurt, was standing alongside and waving a greeting. The Master was sprayed with foam and the pilot given a lift back to dispersal. In the manner of someone who has just fallen off a horse immediately getting up on another one, he demanded another plane at once!

In June 1942 a US Army jeep arrived at the rear entrance to the airfield, probably coming from Wightwick Hall which was occupied by Americans. The passenger who was wearing a leather jacket with no insignia asked to see the Commanding Officer. The ground crew were ordered to prepare a Master III for flight and the visitor flew off in it. Shortly afterwards the timekeeper came running from his office waving the Time and Flight Form. It had been signed by General Mark Clark, soon to be in charge of operations in Italy.

Another distinguished visitor arrived by mistake. A Dominie, the military name for the de Havilland Dragon Rapide, landed, and out stepped two very smart RAF policemen. They asked where they were, and when told it was RAF Perton, they said they had never heard of it. While they were being shown where they were on the map, a tall gentleman in a morning suit and hat stepped out, and introduced himself as Sir Archiebald Sinclair, the Air Minister. Once he had discovered their location the Dominie took off and flew away.

In July 1942 the Masters returned to Tern Hill, and in September were replaced by a flight of Oxfords from Shawbury again. It became almost a self-contained unit, most servicing, except major overhauls, being done in the solitary hangar.

No. 11 Service Training School had been redesignated No. 11 (P) Advanced Flying Unit. It undertook the final multi-engined training of pilots who had received their basic training in the Dominions and America. It was originally intended to be a four-week course, but this had to be greatly extended as the pupils were not used to Black Country weather and the associated navigational problems, especially in the very congested skies of Shropshire and south Staffordshire.

On 28 September 1943 No. 1511 Blind Approach Training Flight arrived at Perton. It was equipped with an unusual mobile Mercury-Sodium flare path, Perton being the first station to use it. The bright yellow 2 kw flares were used in daylight for night-flying training. Pupil pilots wore goggles with special lenses, and had a sodium light on their instrument panel. The amount the pilot could see was variable according to the darkness of the lens, varying from bright moonlight to an effect which simulated total darkness.

This was safer for the pupil than actual night-time flying, if he ever got into trouble he could just whip off the goggles to find out which way up he was. It also meant that the flare path did not have to be lit at night, making it less of a magnet for German bombers.

The RAF Maintenance Squadron at RAF Perton, outside the solitary hangar in August 1944 (Ken Jones)

As a further precaution against air attack Perton was also surrounded by smokescreen pots. Apparently they were rarely lit, for which the nearby inhabitants must have been profoundly grateful. In fact the airfield was never bombed during the war, though a bomb did fall as close as Wood Road in Tettenhall.

The Mercury-Sodium flares were heavy and attached to bomb-type trailers so that they could be towed round the airfield, as there was only one set for the three runways. This had to be done every time the wind changed.

Occasionally the flares were lit at night, as Perton was designated an emergency landing field. Often aircraft that were lost circled overhead until the flares were lit to guide them in. Unfortunately the flares took ten to twenty minutes to warm up, which must have given the odd pilot an anxious wait.

Numerous aircraft landed this way including Wellingtons, Spitfires, Hurricanes and B-17 Fortresses. One Dakota landed several times, mistaking Perton for Ringway, Manchester!

To start with the AFU had three flights at Shawbury, and one each at Perton, Condover and Wheaton Aston, which was very unwieldy. To make it more manageable, on 1 August it was split into two. No. 21 (P) AFU was formed out of it, centred on RAF Little Onn, Wheaton Aston, with Perton as its satellite station. It had seventy-one Oxfords in all, plus two Avro Ansons and one Magister. The initial flying was done at Perton, followed by the Blind Approach Training with the Mercury-Sodium flares, and then final training was done at Wheaton Aston. No. 21 (P) AFU remained the only permanent RAF resident unit until the end of the war, but not the only operator from the airfield.

Helliwells Ltd assembled Douglas Boston and Havoc light bombers at Walsall Airport. As this was only a small grass airfield, the final testing of these aircraft was

A Douglas Boston at RAF Perton, having equipment removed before flying to Pendeford for modifications by Boulton Paul (J. Endean)

done at Perton, which had far more room. Boulton Paul was a 'Mother' company for the Boston and Havoc, and it also used Perton for flight testing because Pendeford did not have paved runways.

Although Perton did have paved runways this did not stop aircraft becoming bogged down on the grass areas at the lower end, near to the hangar. This was no problem for the Oxfords that were relatively light, but on one occasion a B-17 was stuck for two days. In the end it was pulled out by tractors, with planks under the wheels.

On another occasion a B-17 that had landed at Perton by mistake was taking off. Because of a dip in the runway the pilot could not see a lorry containing a number of civilian maintenance men trundling along in the other direction. The Control Tower was rarely manned so the pilots could not be warned by radio.

When they saw the huge B-17 roaring towards them the horrified civilians jumped off the moving truck and ran for their lives. The wing of the bomber clipped the cab of the truck, and the pilot was just able to stop before the end of the runway, with the aileron hanging off. Not surprisingly the language was a little colourful for a while, especially as the Americans were going on leave via Prestwick, and did not appreciate the delay. In the end they repaired the aircraft themselves and took off successfully.

Although none of the Oxfords crashed at Perton, a number at Wheaton Aston did, and the war claimed many of the young men who passed through Perton. Of one group of eight who had a celebration dinner in Tettenhall on the completion of their course, none survived the war. The unit had expanded so much a second satellite at Tatenhill was assigned in February 1944. Despite the crashes the unit almost achieved its full complement of 148 Oxfords. In May 1944 the unit as a whole flew an incredible 10,837 flying hours, but from thenceforth it began to run down.

One of the last wartime visitors to Perton was Pilot Officer J. Douglas of 521 Squadron, stationed at Langhorn, Norfolk. On a day in October 1945, when no other flying was taking place because of the weather, he logged a low-flying exercise in a Hurricane IIc, P2802, and flew to Perton to visit his wife in hospital in West Bromwich. This was actually one of the last batch of 112 Hurricanes to be built, the very last being P2865, now in the Battle of Britain Memorial Flight.

Perton had always been a very quiet posting, but now it became much quieter. Flying did continue for a while; it was a satellite to 21 (P) AFU at Seighford near Stafford until May 1946 when that unit closed. In August Perton was placed on a Care and Maintenance basis, and Wheaton Aston followed in December. On 10 July 1947 Perton was abandoned by the RAF and passed eventually to the Agricultural Land Commission.

The Dutch Camp became a refugee centre for a time, housing Poles, Latvians and Lithuanians. An Auster light aircraft was based at the airfield for a while during the sixties, and when Wolverhampton Airport also closed in 1970 Sir Alfred McAlpine & Sons Ltd wanted to re-open it to base their King Air executive aircraft there, but that was Perton's last fling. It has now disappeared completely from sight under the Perton housing estate.

Apart from a few outbuildings surviving on nearby farms, the only reminder to all the RAF pilots who learned their trade at Perton, is a small memorial, placed on the site of the main runway, next to Sainsbury's supermarket.

27

1946–92, BOULTON PAUL AIRCRAFT: POST-WAR, WOLVERHAMPTON

The end of a world war had drastic consequences once more for the aircraft industry. Contracts were cancelled and there was a large run-down in production. Boulton Paul was lucky to receive a contract to recondition Wellington bombers and convert them to T.10 standard for Flying Training Command, and they became a familiar sight at Pendeford for a while. This contract was augmented with contracts to build turrets for Avro Lincolns and Shackletons.

The one ray of hope for the British aircraft industry as a whole was the jet engine. Advanced though they were, all the piston-engined aircraft that had been built during the war could be rendered obsolete overnight by turbo-jet- and turbo-prop-powered aircraft, and with the destruction of the German aircraft industry it was Britain which led the world in this new technology.

In 1945 the Air Ministry issued Specification T.7/45 for a turbo-prop-powered three-seat advanced trainer to replace the old Master and Harvard. John North had decided that trainer aircraft were best suited to the relative small size of the company. After failing to secure an order for an elementary trainer for Specification T.16/48, for which the de Havilland Chipmunk was the eventual aircraft chosen, he concentrated on this new opportunity. There were two main contenders for this contract, the Avro Athena T.1 and the Boulton Paul P.108 Balliol T.1, both of which were to be powered by the Armstrong Siddeley Mamba turbo-prop engine.

The Mamba was a scaled down Armstrong-Siddeley Python with a straight through gas flow. It was rated at 1,320 h.p., and on the Balliol the exhaust was on the port side aft of the wing, which helped to counteract the torque of the propeller.

The first prototype Balliol, VL892, had to be fitted with a 820 h.p. Bristol Mercury piston engine as a temporary measure, as the Mamba was not ready. The first flight took place on 30 May 1947, at the hands of Robin Lindsay Neale. It was the second prototype, VL917, which had the honour of becoming the world's first single-engined, turbo-prop-powered aircraft when it took to the air on 24 March 1948. The rival Mamba-powered Athena did not fly until 12 June 1948.

The new power-plant was not without its troubles, and on one occasion the Mamba died. Lindsay Neale felt he could make it back to the airfield, but unfortunately the lowered undercarriage just clipped the fence at the Marsh Lane end and the aircraft crashed.

Delays in development of the Mamba engine, and its expense, led to a change of heart by the Air Ministry. There were large numbers of war-surplus Merlin engines and

The first prototype Balliol T.1, VL892, after having its original Mercury engine replaced by a Mamba turbo-prop (Boulton Paul Society)

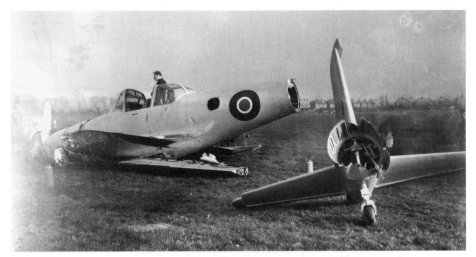

An unfortunate end for the world's first aircraft powered by a single turbo-prop, the second prototype Balliol T.1, VL917. Exeriencing engine trouble Robin Lindsay Neale attempted to make an emergency landing at Pendeford and just clipped the fence (Boulton Paul Society)

Boulton Paul apprentices in June 1951. For those who cannot remember the Wellington T.10 being behind them, this is a composite photograph (Dowty Boulton Paul Ltd)

spares, and in 1947 Specification T.14/47 was issued for a Merlin 35-powered, two-seat advanced trainer, for which both the Balliol and the Athena were redesigned.

Neale had found elevator reversal occurred at around 320 m.p.h. With Peter Tishaw as co-pilot he set out to dive the prototype at over 400 m.p.h. to check the control responses. Unfortunately the windscreen disintegrated, possibly caused by hitting a bird, and the aircraft dived into the ground, hitting a field opposite Lawn Lane Camp at Coven. Both men were killed instantly. Neale was replaced by Fl. Lt. A.E. (Ben) Gunn, who had been testing the Balliol at Boscombe Down.

Boulton Paul's first jet, 'The Yellow Peril'

In 1946 a specification No. E.27/46 was issued for a high speed, delta-winged research aircraft, powered by a Rolls-Royce Nene jet engine. Boulton Paul produced the P.111, which first flew on 6 October 1950. Because Wolverhampton Airport lacked paved runways, testing of jet aircraft associated with Boulton Paul was to be undertaken at Seighford near Stafford, and the company extended the main runway and provided extra hangarage. Just before this there was also a brief use of the Royal Radar Establishment's airfield at Defford.

The P.111 had a 5,100 lb Nene, and a leading edge sweep for the delta wing of 45 degrees. It appeared at both the Paris and Farnborough Air Shows of 1951. In 1953 it was modified with four air brakes fitted behind the cockpit, and was then redesignated the P.111A. At the same time its silver paintwork was replaced with an all-yellow scheme, with black trim. Almost inevitably it acquired the nick-name 'Yellow Peril'.

It began an extensive research programme at RAE Bedford which finished in June 1958. It was capable of Mach 0.93 (650 m.p.h.) in level flight at 35,000 ft. Once its flying days were over it was used as an instructional airframe at the College of Aeronautics, Cranwell, for many years, before moving nearer home to the Midland Air Museum at Coventry Airport.

The Black Widow-maker

A further development of the P.111A, the P.120, first flew on 6 August 1952, piloted by A.E. (Ben) Gunn, Boulton Paul's chief test pilot. It had a re-designed fin and a high mounted all-moving tailplane. Its ominous all-black paint scheme earned it the nick-name 'Black Widow-maker', which was to prove very prophetic.

On its very first flight it consumed an alarming amount of Boscombe Down's runway before clawing its way into the air, just above the heads of some startled agricultural workers outside the airfield boundary. The problem was the tailplane setting, but once in the air it proved quite pleasant to handle. The powered controls had no feedback system, and on 28 August, after only 11 hours of flying the P.120 crashed because of this.

As he was flying along the south coast at about 5,000 ft, Gunn heard a loud buzz,

The P.111 in the air over Wiltshire (Boulton Paul Society)

The P.111A preserved at the Midland Air Museum, Coventry, with members of the Boulton Paul Society, many of whom helped build it

A.E. 'Ben' Gunn undertaking taxiing trials in the P.111, VT935, on Pendeford's grass runways. The first flight was at Boscombe Down (Dowty Boulton Paul Ltd)

and then there was a heart-stopping bang. The P.120 began a series of rolls to port, which he was only able to correct with full opposite rudder and stick. He pulled out of the resulting dive using the tailplane trimmer. An intense flutter had developed in the port elevon, unknown to Gunn, and a hinge had eventually failed.

He fought for half an hour using the remaining elevon, and the trimming tailplane, to control the aircraft, steering it towards the long runway at Boscombe Down, but it became obvious that even a wheels-up landing would be impossible. When he jettisoned the canopy the P.120 went into a roll, and though he tried to eject immediately, the aircraft was upside-down when he did so. By mistake he pulled the parachute ripcord before jettisoning the seat, and this saved his life as he crashed through some trees just as the parachute opened. The P.120 ploughed into Salisbury Plain. Gunn had the dubious distinction of being the first pilot to eject from a delta-wing aircraft.

Amazingly a P.120 tailplane still survives, but not the one fitted when Ben Gunn took to the silk over Wiltshire. A test specimen was kept in the Hatfield Technical College for many years and has now gone to the Midland Air Museum, a fitting companion to the P.111A.

The P.120, VT951, still unpainted, at Boscombe Down

The P.120 in its all-black paint scheme just before its crash (Boulton Paul Society)

Producing the Balliol

Production hopes were centred on the Merlin-powered Balliol. Once more it was the Balliol prototype, VW897, which was first in the air on 10 July 1948, followed by the first Merlin-powered Athena on 1 August. Three more Balliol prototypes, redesignated the T.2 were also constructed, and then a contract was placed for seventeen pre-production aircraft for service trials. Two of these, from the Central Flying School, gave a display of aerobatics at the 1950 RAF display at Farnborough. The prototype Balliol T.2 had flown at the 1948 Farnborough Show, giving an impressive performance compared with the Mercury-powered Balliol 1 which had been displayed at the SBAC Show at Radlett, the previous year.

The control reversal problems were solved by altering the tailplane incidence, and strengthening it. The 1,245 h.p. Merlin 35 gave the Balliol T.2 a top speed of 288 m.p.h. at 9,000 ft and a ceiling of 32,500 ft. It was armed with a single .303 Browning machine gun in the port wing and provision for two 60 lb rockets under each wing.

Large contracts were placed for the Balliol, and Blackburns were also to subcontract it, but the Air Ministry had a further change of heart. The Ministry decided that it was more appropriate to have a jet aircraft as an advanced trainer, and the Vampire T.11 was ordered for this role, and Balliol contracts were substantially reduced. Boulton Paul was to build 132 T.2s at Wolverhampton, and Blackburn only 30.

The first production aircraft, WF989, first flew in April 1952, and only one Flying Training School, No. 7 at Cottesmore, was equipped with them. Subsequently they went to 288 Squadron for radar training duties at Middle Wallop and 228 OCUs at North Luffenham to fly as targets for Brigand 5s. Others were used as station 'hacks' and for refresher flying by senior officers. It later served at the RAF College Cranwell.

Meanwhile the Royal Navy had a requirement for a deck-landing trainer, and Boulton Paul redesigned the Balliol with a strengthened undercarriage, folding wings, and an arrester hook. The prototype was a converted pre-production Balliol T.2, VR599, which flew in October 1952 and a total of thirty were ordered, designated Sea Balliol T.21s. The last was delivered on 7 December 1954. Three later served at the RAE Bedford, and one of these, WL732, has been preserved at the Cosford Aerospace Museum.

Other work undertaken by the company as Balliol production went ahead included test work on Gust-Alleviation using a modified Lancaster. The electronic power controls simulated gusts and the ailerons counteracted them by both moving up together. The Lancaster, with its long probe attached to the nose, operated from Pendeford, usually flown by Ben Gunn.

The company also did work on Vampires for de Havillands. New intakes were installed on a Rolls-Royce, Nene-powered Vampire. The aircraft flew into Pendeford and had the intakes modified, before flying out for continued tests elsewhere. Nene-powered Vampires were ordered in large numbers by Australia and Switzerland. Another Vampire, VV630, was fitted for target towing, and VX 985 had a survey unit fitted.

Boulton Paul had its own Balliol demonstrator, with civil registration G-ANSF, which flew for the first time on 23 August 1954, and was demonstrated at Farnborough

Boulton Paul apprentices in 1954, in front of a production Balliol (Boulton Paul Society)

A production Sea Balliol making a low pass above the taxiway to the factory, with Pendeford
Farm on the hill behind

One of the few jets to use Pendeford's grass runways – a Nene-powered DH Vampire, TG270,
with new intakes designed by Boulton Paul (Dowty Boulton Paul Ltd)

that year. Only one further order for the Balliol was forthcoming however. The Ceylon Air Force ordered twelve, the first being delivered in April 1955 and the last in August 1957. They received the Ceylon A.F. serials CA301–CA312.

The last Balliol T.2, CA310, is preserved at the home of the No. 4 Helicopter Air Wing at Katunayake in Sri Lanka.

Powered flying controls

The Balliol was the very last complete aircraft built by Boulton Paul, though it was an earlier design than the P.111A and the P.120, but the company was already prospering in other areas. The coming of the jet aircraft had meant that powered flying controls were needed, as pilots could not manually operate controls against the huge forces involved. With the knowledge gained in designing and building electro-hydraulic turrets, John North and Boulton Paul became pioneers of powered control systems.

The very first Boulton Paul powered flying control systems were installed in the Saunders-Roe Princess, the last of the giant flying boats. Others were fitted to the Valiant, Canberra and Vulcan bombers, the BAC.111 and VC-10 airliners, and a whole series of subsequent aircraft such as the Lightning and Buccaneer. A great deal of test work was done, particularly on Canberras, with different systems, especially in trying to give pilots the same sort of 'feel' as a simple mechanical control used to give.

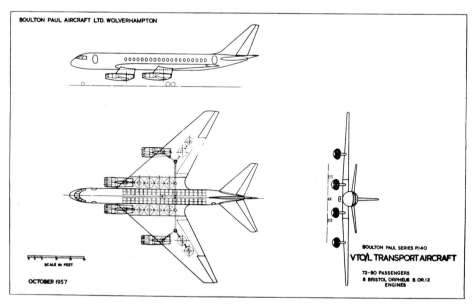

A drawing of the P.140 VTOL 72–80 passenger airliner with eight Bristol Orpheus engines and fan lift, dating from 1957 (Dowty Boulton Paul Ltd)

The Boulton Paul P.122 rocket-propelled interceptor project of 1954 (Boulton Paul Society)

Boulton Paul used its Seighford facility for development and overhaul work on a number of RAF aircraft. A Javelin Mk.1, XA562, from the first production batch, was used as a trials aircraft with a Rolls-Royce Avon RA.24 installation. A large number of Canberras and later Lightnings were overhauled there, with many trial installations being undertaken. Nine Canberra B.2s were converted to T.11s. The T.11 was a Target Interception Trainer, and had a lengthened nose to carry the radar. A Boulton Paul four-cannon pack was fitted to interdiction Canberras and the modification of the B.15 to carry Nord AS-30 missiles was also carried out at Seighford. Eventually the British Aircraft Corporation began retaining such work for its own divisions.

The company became a subcontractor for Beagle Aircraft and built the wings and nacelles for the Beagle 206 light twin, known as the Basset in RAF service, and undertook the structural testing of the Basset fuselage.

It was also natural that Boulton Paul should diversify into industrial hydraulics and such areas as pressing body panels for the motor industry. In 1961 John North, now Chairman of the company, proposed a merger with the Dowty Group of Companies, and this went ahead.

Dowty Aerospace, Wolverhampton, is now one of the world's leading companies in the design and production of hydraulic systems, and in particular it has been at the

The last Boulton Paul aircraft ever to fly, the Sea Balliol T.21, WL732, now preserved at the Aerospace Museum, Cosford (Dowty Boulton Paul Ltd)

forefront of innovation in fly-by-wire systems. As early as 1956 it provided the very first electrically-signalled control system to fly, on a Tay-engined Vickers Viscount. It provided such systems for Concorde, and on that aircraft alone has clocked up more fly-by-wire mileage than all its competitors. Its systems are currently to be found on the Tornado, Jaguar, Airbus, BAe 146, Agusta A129 and AM-X.

Boulton Paul was never one of the giants of the aircraft industry, never a de Havilland or an Avro, but its history has been a reflection of the industry in general. Even by stretching the meaning of the phrase to its limit, only half a dozen of its own aircraft ever went into production, and only the Defiant and Balliol in any numbers, but it has made a substantial contribution to British aviation.

28

1946–55, WALSALL AIRPORT: POST-WAR

After the war, Helliwells' contract for the Harvard continued until 1956, and work continued on Havocs for a while. Work on the Harvards was increasingly refurbishing them, but for the Havocs it was largely to scrap them.

To replace the Havoc work Helliwells won a Cat.B contract for Seafires. Aircraft brought by road from storage were completely refurbished and put into the air. Though they took off from Walsall, the exigencies of war no longer applied, and pilots were not forced to try and land high-speed fighters on such a tiny strip. The Seafires were flown to Castle Bromwich for any further work.

The company operated a number of their own aircraft from the airport, including two Tiger Moths, G-AHZA and G-AHKZ, a Globe Swift G-AHUV and a Proctor G-AHGT.

Other civilian flying continued at the airport in a desultory manner, and Kenning Airways operated there for a short while in 1947. Private owners used the airfield of course, including R.M. Smith and J.L. Brockhouse, who kept the Taylorcraft Plus Cs, G-AFUA and G-AFUB there. The former was wrecked beyond repair on 18 October 1948.

The Council reviewed the operation of the airport in 1948, but decided to renew Helliwells lease for another ten years. A number of component contracts were won, including the nacelles for the Avro Ashton jet airliner, and the Harvard contract continued. The last one to be refurbished, KF448, flew away in 1956, and shortly afterwards aircraft servicing ceased and then Helliwells moved entirely to Elmdon. The airfield closed for flying, and was leased to a sports club. The last aircraft in residence was a derelict Hawk Major, G-ADAB.

There is little doubt that Walsall Airport was ill-sited, and always too small for anything but light aircraft. With Castle Bromwich, Pendeford, and later Elmdon, only short distances away, it was always fighting for survival, but strangely, in a way, it has survived two of them. Pendeford and Castle Bromwich have disappeared under housing, but Walsall is still all there to be seen. The club buildings, and Helliwells' hangars are still standing, and in use for other purposes, and the only things to block the well-trimmed grass are the stumps of cricket matches in summer, and goal-posts in winter.

If a Tiger Moth were to land, the scene would be transported back to those optimistic days in the thirties, when hopes were high, and anything seemed possible. But standing in the centre of the field, one wonders at those Douglas Havoc pilots, as they opened the throttle as wide as they could before releasing the brakes, and saying a little prayer.

29
1946–70, WOLVERHAMPTON AIRPORT: POST-WAR AND CLOSURE

Civil flying did not resume at Wolverhampton Airport until 1 January 1946 with the lifting of government restrictions. The Midland Aero Club did not return but the Wolverhampton Aero Club was formed and used, initially, some ex-RAF Miles Magisters. This was rather strange as the twenty-eight EFTS at Wolverhampton still had to use old biplane Tiger Moths.

Wolverhampton Aviation, which was part of Air Schools Ltd, as was Derby Aviation, ran the airport and became a Miles service agent. When Miles Aircraft went out of business in 1948 Wolverhampton Aviation acquired six uncompleted twin-engined Geminis plus two incomplete sets of parts and ten sets of wings, for use as Messenger spares. The six Geminis were completed from these parts and fitted with Gipsy Major engines, and sold between 1950 and 1952. It could be said that the airport hosted two aircraft manufacturers for that short period of time. A further ten Cirrus-powered Geminis were converted to Gipsy Major engines.

The Air Schools fleet was shared between Derby and Wolverhampton, as required, and when the Wolverhampton Aero Club was sold in August 1955, it included eight Austers, eight Magisters and two Geminis, as well as three Rapides for airline work.

King's Cup Air Race

In 1950 the famous King's Cup Air Race came to Wolverhampton, for the first and only time. The handicap race was over three laps of a 100 km course, with the hope that nine 100 km closed-circuit world records would be broken, or set for the first time, several classes having been newly instituted. The course was via Abbots Bromley to Meir, near Stoke, with the last turn at Pave Lane, Newport.

The King's Cup was held on 17 June, after a small air display, with the Goodyear Trophy Race the following day. The air display was opened by a formation flight by aircraft of the 25 Reserve Flying School, and then there was a Seafire formation display from the Naval Air Station at Bramcote. Ron Porteous flew the experimental Auster fitted with a castoring undercarriage, and Ben Gunn displayed a Balliol.

The first aircraft away in the King's Cup were the Comper Swift, G-ABUS, flown by R.E. Clear, and Henry Moss in his own Mosscraft, G-AEST, a single-seat monoplane. Five seconds later another Comper Swift took off, flown by a Wolverhampton Aero Club member, 22-year-old A.L. Cole. There were three women in the 36-strong field including Mrs M. Rendell, flying, amazingly, a de Havilland Rapide. The last of the totally civilian aircraft to take off was a director of Wolverhampton Aviation, Ron Paine, in his Miles Hawk Speed Six, who had come second in the previous year's King's Cup at Castle Bromwich, and was therefore one of the favourites.

The scratch aircraft was a Spitfire VB flown by the third of the women, Miss R.M. Sharpe, 54 minutes 55 seconds behind the first aircraft off, and just behind a Spitfire Trainer flown by P.G. Robarts. One of the most interesting entrants took off just before the Spitfire Trainer. The last Hawker Hurricane built, G-AMAU (PZ865), was entered in a silver and blue colour scheme by Princess Margaret, flown by a certain Group Captain Townsend.

Unfortunately Henry Moss crashed his Mosscraft while turning at the Newport pylon. His wing-tip touched the ground, despite the 600 ft minimum height stipulation, and he was killed.

The handicapper did his job very well, because at the finish a whole gaggle of light aircraft appeared from the direction of Courtaulds, many of them diving in order to pick up a little extra speed in a frantic finish. Suddenly the Hurricane appeared from nowhere going like the wind, and overhauling everything, except the Miles Hawk trainer of Edward Day, who won the race with Group Captain Townsend only 50 or 60 yards behind in second place.

The sky was now full of aircraft all trying to land, and there was an unfortunate accident when Miss Sharpe clipped the tail of a taxiing aircraft as she was landing the Spitfire, but no one was hurt.

Five new 100 km closed-circuit records were set, two of them breaking old records, and three setting records in new classes. They were, with the old records – where applicable – in brackets:

Class C.1a – A.L. Cole (Comper Swift) 126.22 m.p.h.
Class C.1b – R.R. Paine (Hawk Speed Six) 192.83 m.p.h. (163.4)
Class C.1c – P.G. Robarts (Spitfire Tr.) 328.48 m.p.h. (322.79)
Class C.1d – Miss R.M. Sharpe (Spitfire) 322.79 m.p.h.
Class C.1e – P.G. Robarts (Spitfire Tr.) 328.48 m.p.h.

On the following day a crowd of only a few hundred, despite the free entry, saw the Goodyear Trophy Race won in an even more exciting finish. After two heats around the 21¼ mile course via Wheaton Aston and Penkridge, D. Lowry won the final in his Chrislea Skyjeep, by only three-quarters of a length from N. Somers in a Miles Gemini, with A.L. Cole, in his Comper Swift third. Incredibly only 10 seconds covered the first ten finishers.

Don Everall Aviation

In September 1951 an Elmdon-based airline, Lees-Hill Aviation, which operated two de Havilland Rapides and two Auster light aircraft, was taken over by Modern Air Transport to create Don Everall (Aviation) Ltd. Don Everall, of course, was a well-known Wolverhampton coach operator.

Wolverhampton Airport in its heyday. Don Everall (Aviation) Ltd's staff with some of the fleet ranged behind them, including a DC-3 which was serviced at Wolverhampton, though operating mainly from Birmingham Airport (Eric Holden)

Eric Holden was recruited as chief engineer to start the maintenance set-up from scratch with Johnny Atkinson as the chief pilot. It operated as an airline from Elmdon, with services to the Isle of Man and the Channel Islands, as well as charters. On 7 October 1955 one of the Rapides, G-AGLR, on a charter from Paris to Birmingham crash-landed on a Berkswell golf course, but the pilot and all eight passengers escaped the resulting fire.

The Channel Islands flights in particular were very successful, and on one notable day a Rapide operated four return trips, each one taking 4½ hours! A further service was started to Bembridge on the Isle of Wight, but they began having difficulty finding Rapide-qualified pilots, and started looking at bigger aircraft to take the strain.

In 1957 Don Everall bought their first DC-3, G-ANEG, from Transair. This operated most of their scheduled services from Birmingham, as well as the new inclusive tour flights. Independent airlines had discovered that they could operate to foreign destinations provided they included hotel rooms in the fare. Don Everall (Aviation) co-operated with the tour operator, Transglobe, to begin inclusive tours to Palma, Perpignan and Basel. In 1959 'NEG was joined by another DC-3, G-AMSF, which enabled the company to serve further IT destinations.

Scheduled flights from Wolverhampton

In 1953 Wolverhampton had finally got a scheduled air service. Derby Aviation began a summer service from Derby Airport via Wolverhampton to Jersey, stopping at Birmingham Airport for Customs clearance. On 18 July the first service was flown by a de Havilland Rapide, G-AEAL. The service was on Saturdays and Sundays, scheduled to leave Wolverhampton at 8.45 a.m. and the return fare was only £12.

In February 1953 Don Everall (Aviation) also acquired a licence to operate a scheduled service from Wolverhampton to Ronaldsway on the Isle of Man. The service was also flown by Rapides, but did not survive very long.

The Derby Aviation service continued with Rapides the following summer, and then on 5 May 1955 a DC-3 Dakota flew the route for the first time. It was a short-lived honour for the town, however, because the stop at Wolverhampton was dropped from the service in 1957.

When Derby Aviation's operation of Wolverhampton Airport came to an end in 1955 Don Everall (Aviation) took it over. From then on all major servicing of the Rapides and DC-3s was undertaken at Wolverhampton. The DC-3s even operated a few lightweight charter flights from Wolverhampton, such as taking a plane-load of farmers to Blackpool.

A Don Everall charter flight, full of scouts, about to leave the airport. Captain Johnny Atkinson (second left) later became Sir Alfred McAlpine & Son's pilot, operating a Beech Queen Air from the airport (Eric Holden)

The Man in the Sky

Wolverhampton Airport even made the silver screen in the fifties. In April 1956 a Jack Hawkins film *The Man in the Sky* was made at Pendeford, all the flying sequences being filmed there and internal shots with a mock-up aircraft being filmed in one of the hangars. The Bristol Freighter, which featured heavily in the film, almost came to grief when it skidded into a ditch. It was one of Jack Hawkins' more obscure efforts, but one to watch out for on the late night schedules.

On 5 March 1960 Don Everall's DC-3, G-AMSF, on a Jersey-bound flight crashed on take-off from Birmingham, and only missed one of the hangars by a few feet. It was replaced in May by a Vickers Viking, G-AKBG, and a week later another Viking, G-AMNL, was added to the fleet. This aircraft was lost off Crete while on a cargo flight in August.

Don Everall's airline division was bought out in January 1961 by a Gatwick-based airline, Air Safaris Ltd, on whose board was Mr P. Everall. Financial problems caused this airline to close twelve months later, and its licences were revoked.

Don Everall (Aviation) continued to operate at Wolverhampton Airport, however, and in 1961 its aircraft consisted of four Austers, two Autocrats, G-AHAP and G-AIJZ, and two Alphas, G-AHST and G-AIBZ, and also two Tiger Moths G-ANJK and G-ANME. This was a fleet typical of many small airport operators, old British tail-draggers, museum pieces by contemporary American standards. Modern American

Part of the Don Everall fleet in formation over the Staffordshire countryside (Eric Holden)

A familiar sight both during and after the war. In this case club member, Bill Cambridge, poses with two Don Everall Tiger Moths (Eric Holden)

Cessnas and Pipers were not yet to be seen because of import restrictions, but British light-aircraft manufacturers, cocooned by this shield, were about to face the chill winds of competition.

In July 1961 Don Everall (Aviation) acquired its first Piper aircraft, a PA-22 Colt, G-ARNI, with a modern tricycle undercarriage and a Lycoming 0-235-CIB engine. The Colt was not a completely modern all-metal design, it still had fabric covering, but it was a big improvement on even the Austers let alone the old Tiger Moths. Another Colt, G-ARON, followed in 1962, together with an all-metal thoroughly modern Piper PA-28 Cherokee 160, G-ARVR.

By 1965 both Tiger Moths and all but one of the old Austers had gone, and the fleet had been augmented with another Colt, G-ARKP, a four-seat version, the Piper Caribbean 150, G-ARIL, and a Cessna 172F, G-ATBT. Strangely Don Everall also bought two of the latest Auster Terriers, G-ASYG and G-ASZE, to complement the last Alpha, G-AHST.

A number of interesting aircraft were hangared at Wolverhampton over the years. Boulton Paul operated its own Airspeed Oxford, G-AHTW, for many years, and in 1964 this was preserved by the Skyfame Museum. It is now on display at the Duxford Historic Aviation Centre wearing its RAF serial V3388, a link with both Pendeford and the Oxfords which flew at RAF Perton.

The airport buildings from the air during the 1960s (note the Piper aircraft now added to the Don Everall fleet) (Eric Holden)

A Skyways Avro 748 bringing a party of French government officials and industrialists to Pendeford to visit the Boulton Paul Factory in connection with the Concorde programme (Dowty Boulton Paul Ltd)

One of the more unusual visitors to the airport, a Pfalz D.III replica *en route* to Ireland for filming of *The Blue Max* (Eric Holden)

Mr Peter Bannister was a well-known private owner at the airport, initially with his little Tipsy Nipper, G-APYB, in which he won the King's Cup Air Race. Obviously having developed a taste for air racing he then bought an amazing Kensinger KF, G-ASSV, a home-built single-seat racing aircraft from America. Between 1969 and 1972 he rebuilt almost entirely from scratch the Cosmic Wind, G-ARUL, which had crashed at Halfpenny Green on 29 August 1966.

Another unusual aircraft at Pendeford for some time was the Chrislea CH.3 Super Ace, G-AKVF, owned by Mr D.L. Rugg-Easey. The Super Ace had been an attempt to build a modern British light aircraft, which failed. Owners preferred cheap, ex-wartime aircraft such as the Messengers, or Auster variants, like the J.5L, G-APVG, also hangared there. A Druine D.5 Turbi, G-APFA, owned by the Wolverhampton Ultra Light Flying Group, was another uncommon sight in Pendeford's hangars.

Crossroads at Pendeford

Filming returned to Pendeford in 1967 when ATV brought Noele Gordon and the *Crossroads* cast to the airport to shoot some scenes, in which club members featured in the background, as the 'Crossroads Trophy' was awarded as part of the story line. Stan

Noele Gordon, with a background cast of flying club members filming an episode of *Crossroads* at the airport (Eric Holden)

Stennet, a later *Crossroads* actor, was a frequent visitor to the airport operating his own aircraft.

There were numerous air displays at the airport in the post-war period, perhaps typical of them was the Royal Air Force Association Display on 26 June 1965. Those who attended were amazed to find the giant shape of a Blackburn Beverley transport standing on the airfield. That the pilot managed to squeeze it onto Pendeford's short grass runway is a testament to its short-field performance. Apparently the pilot made some pointed comments about just how short it was!

The items were typical of such displays, a series of different RAF current types: Comet II, Chipmunk, Sycamore, Lightning, Hunter, Jet Provost, Victor and Shackleton; plus two aerobatic teams, three Jet Provosts from Syerston and the Red Arrows, then flying Gnats.

There was not the variety of vintage aircraft on the air-show circuit that there is now, but Hurricane G-AMAU, the last one built, and the second place finisher in the 1950 King's Cup at Wolverhampton, was by then owned by Hawker-Siddeley and was flown in the display by their chief test pilot, Bill Bedford. The Tiger Club provided much of

The biggest aircraft ever to land and take off from Wolverhampton Airport, a Blackburn Beverley during the 1965 RAFA Air Display (Eric Holden)

the rest of the display: a Stampe flown by Neil Williams; the delightful Arrow Active biplane flown by the current National Air Racing Champion, Dennis Hartis; and 'Lolita' standing on the wing of a Tiger Moth.

The Chrisair Parachute Display Team provided the obligatory free-fall parachute display, and that was all. In a way it was little different from the display which had opened the airport just twenty-seven years earlier, apart from the noise level, that is!

The closure of the airport

The writing was on the wall for Don Everall (Aviation) and the airport however, and it was being written by the Borough's Public Works and Estates Committee. In 1967 they recommended the closure of the airport once Don Everall's agreement had expired in 1971. The one obstacle blocking the way was Boulton Paul's flying rights, which did not expire until the year 2035.

Closure was recommended despite the fact that use of the airport had steadily increased, from 640 movements in 1959 to 2,116 in 1966, plus over 20,000 instructional flights. The 1966 movements included business aircraft from fifty different companies coming from ninety-seven different airfields.

A similar proposal to close the airport had been made in 1961, and the possibility of replacing it with a new airport near Gailey island or at Halfpenny Green had been explored, but eventually rejected. Now that Halfpenny Green had been opened for private flying by a private company, the Council's case was far stronger: many of the private owners having moved to Halfpenny Green anyway. It was financial exigencies which had prompted the call for closure, the Council claimed that the airport was losing ratepayers' money, and it was also valuable building land, but safety was to be dramatically added to the arguments of those who wanted closure.

On 9 April 1970 a de Havilland Dove 8, G-AVHV, registered to Dowty Group Services flying in to collect Boulton Paul directors, crashed on approach to the airport. It hit a house in Redhurst Drive, Fordhouses, and both crew and one occupant of the house died. Though this was the first fatal crash, other accidents were quoted to illustrate the dangers of having an airport so near a built-up area.

In July 1952 an instructor and pupil were injured when a Miles Hawk Trainer 3, G-AHNV, force-landed outside the perimeter fence. In September 1958 the propellers of an Air Survey DC-3 touched the ground while the pilot was indulging himself in a very low pass, but the aircraft landed safely. Finally in September 1965 Don Everall's

The sad end for Piper Cherokee G-ARVR, after crashing into the Shropshire Union Canal with carburettor icing (Eric Holden)

Cherokee, G-ARVR, crashed into the canal on take-off, without really becoming airborne, due to carburettor-icing, and the three occupants were injured.

Even fears that the airport would be used by jet aircraft, with the resulting noise, were quoted as reasons for closing it. As far as is known the only jets ever to land on what was an exclusively grass airfield were a Miles M.77 Sparrowjet (powered by two little Palas engines) in 1956, and a few years earlier a de Havilland Vampire, which Boulton Paul duly converted to Nene-power before it flew out again. Boulton Paul did do taxiing tests with the P.111 at Wolverhampton, which must have been fairly noisy for all concerned, but jets operating from grass strips are rare events, especially ones as prone to bog as Pendeford.

Even as the Council was trying to close the airport a BEA subsidiary, British Air Services, was announcing the creation of a network of scheduled services covering twenty-two towns and cities across Britain, including Wolverhampton. This 'Third Level' operation was to be flown by a passenger version of the Short Skyvan, dubbed Skyliner, and a number of proving flights were undertaken. In the event the scheme was abandoned, and this possible eleventh-hour saviour for the airport evaporated.

The Council agreed to close the airport on 31 December 1970, and asked Boulton Paul to waive its flying rights. The company was to claim compensation, but its case was weakened by the fact that it no longer needed an airfield from which to fly the aircraft it built, and had to use Seighford for test-work with the jet aircraft for which it undertook modifications.

Wolverhampton Aero Club closed on that date, but several private flyers kept their aircraft there at their own risk for some time afterwards. Eventually the Council forced them to vacate, and the last aircraft present was an unairworthy Miles Messenger 2A, G-AHUI, which had been withdrawn from use in September 1960, when owned by E.C. Francis. Perhaps it is appropriate that this was the last of a long line of Miles aircraft to use Pendeford. It eventually had its wings sawn off and went to the Air Scouts in Wharf Street, Wolverhampton, from where the fuselage was rescued by the Cranfield Historic Aircraft Society. It may have been the last fixed-wing aircraft within the town.

Home-built aircraft

The last but one aircraft built in Wolverhampton was the Currie Wot biplane, G-AVEY, built at his home by Mr Keith Sedgewick, who had previously been employed by both Boulton Paul and Wolverhampton Aviation Ltd. This little aircraft had been designed by J.R. Currie, the ground engineer at Lympne airport, in 1937. It had unstaggered wings of 22 ft 1 in span, and was powered by an Aeronca-JAP flat-twin, developing 45 h.p. Two were built before the war, but were destroyed by enemy action at Lympne.

It was revived as a home-built design after the war, and one was even fitted with a Rover gas-turbine engine. Mr Sedgewick's had some modern improvements, with a Pobjoy R radial engine, and was redesignated by him, a Super Wot. Its first flight was on 10 January 1971. It is still extant, owned by Mr A. Eastelow, and based at Dunkeswell airfield in Devon.

Another home-built, a Luton L.A.4A Minor was built in Stourbridge, and registered G-ATKH in June 1968. It was powered by an Aeronca-JAP 40 h.p. engine. The very last aircraft built in the Black Country was a Taylor J.T.1 monoplane, built by David Bateman of Wolverhampton with the help of Keith Sedgewick, who made the first test flight on 6 June 1975. Unfortunately, David Bateman later died in his little aircraft, when it spun in from a height of only 600 ft over Penn.

Either the Hartill or Star monoplanes of 1910 were the first aircraft built in the Black Country, both of wood and fabric construction, with engines of no more than 40 h.p., and open cockpits for their single occupants. Things seemed to have come full circle once again, except that the Super Wot and the Taylor monoplanes, also wood and fabric single-seaters with less than 40 h.p., were rather more efficient flying machines.

Conclusions

All signs of the airport have disappeared now, as it is slowly turned into a housing estate and a Business Park. By a strange quirk of fate one of the opponents of closure,

The final act. The author removing the airport sign in 1974, with the Council's permission, now the only physical evidence that there ever was an airport at Wolverhampton (Peter Brew)

A reminder of Pendeford's heyday, the staff of Air Schools Ltd in 1945, arrayed with two of their huge fleet of Tiger Moths in front of the original hangar. The RAF officer in the centre was the CO of the Station, and on his left is Ron Paine (P.R. Johnson)

Alfred McAlpine Ltd, who had kept the Beech Queen Air, G-ASIU, at the airport, and wanted to continue to do so, is the first occupant of the Business Park.

The last full stop to the airport's story was when the Council granted me permission to remove the airport sign from the main gate, for preservation at the Midland Air Museum in Coventry.

30

1907–92, COMPONENT MANUFACTURERS ROUND THE BLACK COUNTRY

Accles & Pollock, Oldbury

Strictly speaking Accles & Pollock should be listed as aircraft manufacturers as it built Lt. Seddon's *Mayfly* in 1910, but as it never left the ground maybe that is overstating the case. Certainly it provided steel tube for aircraft including the *Mayfly*, dating from Howard Wright's helicopter of 1907 to the present day.

It has been claimed that every single aircraft built in Britain during the Second World War contained Accles & Pollock steel tube, an achievement which it is hard to believe that any other company could equal.

Goodyear Tyre & Rubber Company, Wolverhampton

Goodyear came to Wolverhampton in 1927, and made its first tyre on 15 December. Its Aviation Division provided tyres, wheels and brakes for aircraft, as well as other rubber-based components, and anti-skid braking systems. Just a few of the aircraft fitted by Goodyear were the Viscount, Herald, Carvair, and Accountant.

In addition, the Goodyear company has also been associated with the operation of aircraft over Wolverhampton, most notably the Goodyear Airship, *Europa*. *Europa* was constructed at Cardington in 1972, with 202,700 cu. ft capacity, and powered by two 210 h.p. Continental engines, giving a maximum speed of 50 m.p.h.

Shortly afterwards the airship took employees and guests on a series of flights over the town, and further over the Black Country, from a starting point at RAF Cosford. This was a fitting reminder of a number of airships that have flown over the area. There was Stanley Spencer's airship over Stourbridge in 1905, E.T. Willows' *City of Cardiff* flying from Wolverhampton to Birmingham, the R.34 saluting its engine manufacturers, Sunbeam, and in the 1930s the famous appearance of the *Graf Zeppelin*. The sequence continues, with the Fuji Film airship, built by Airship Industries, being hangared at Halfpenny Green in June 1989, just outside the Black Country, and a further echo of those earlier flights.

The *Graf Zeppelin* in particular has been well remembered by many in the area, both for its looming size and the reminder that it represented the wartime Zeppelin bombing raids. Following the LMS railway line from the north-west, it was seen at Kingswood by a youth who was to become my father, and – over the Willenhall Road in Wolverhampton – was pointed out to a little girl who was to become my mother. Amazingly she could not see this giant apparition in the sky that had such a dramatic effect on many in the Black Country.

As well as operating the Miles Gemini G-AKGE from Pendeford, Goodyear also operated a most unusual aircraft from there for a while, an amphibious Grumman Duck.

H.M. Hobsons/Lucas Aerospace, Wolverhampton

Beginning with their first factory in Cousins Street and expanding to their existing premises on the Stafford Road, Hobsons was world famous for its aircraft carburettors, which it began manufacturing during the First World War. Hobsons provided the Claudel-Hobson carburettors on Alcock and Brown's Vickers Vimy, which made the first non-stop Atlantic crossing by an aircraft. It then provided the carburettors for the R.34 airship, which made the first double crossing shortly afterwards.

During the early thirties, in co-operation with Bristol Aero-Engines it developed the Automatic Boost Control, first fitted to the Bristol Pegasus. This soon led to the development of the Hobson-Penn Automatic Mixture Control. The final outcome of this work was the H.M. Hobson Master Control Injection Carburettor, the most sophisticated such instrument available, even to the present day.

The original small, oil pressure-operated mechanism of the Automatic Boost Control was the birth of the Hobson power-control work, and after the Second World War Hobsons began to develop flap and slat operating systems, and other power actuators. Its systems were applied to many aircraft including BAC.111, HS.125, Caravelle, Trident and Tornado. Carburettors were still produced, of course, most notably for the host of Alvis Leonides-powered aircraft, such as the Percival Provost, Westland Widgeon, and Bristol Sycamore, but this work has inevitably died away.

When taken over by Lucas Aerospace, Hobsons became its Actuation Division, and there were many more applications for its products, including the European Airbus, Fiat G.222, and Saab J-29.

It has also become involved in a joint programme with MBB Helicopter Systems and IPTN Indonesian Aircraft Industry to develop a gun turret for the Bo.105 helicopter. A chin turret armed with a 0.5 inch Browning machine gun, it is sighted by a Ferranti helmet-pointing system.

Marston-Palmer Ltd, Wolverhampton

The small concentration of aerospace manufacturers in the Fordhouses area of Wolverhampton, which includes Lucas Aerospace, Turners, and Dowty Aerospace, also contains Marston-Palmer. It manufactures aircraft heat exchangers, and engine rings, hydraulic components for aerospace applications, and bulk liquid storage facilities for aircraft.

Bolkow Bo 105 helicopter fitted with a Lucas Aerospace 0.5 in gun turret, controlled by a helmet mounted sight

Turner Manufacturing, Wolverhampton

In 1934 Turner acquired a licence to manufacture hydraulic and pneumatic undercarriages of German design. It went on to design its own, and in the Second World War it was one of three approved suppliers. Among its products were tail wheels for Ansons, Lancasters and Blenheims.

After the war Turner returned to making car components, but in 1954 it began making parts for the Rolls-Royce Dart engine, and also Westland helicopter rotor heads, tail rotors and undercarriages. The Rolls-Royce contract was completed but it still made Westland parts.

The company was taken over to become the Spicer Transmission Division, but still making aircraft components.

Other manufacturers

In an area renowned for its metal-bashing industries it is inevitable that numerous companies should be supplying parts for the aircraft industry beyond those already mentioned. For instance, during the Second World War John Thompson Ltd, of Wolverhampton, built rudder components, and exhaust systems for Wellington bombers, and later sub-assemblies for the Meteor jet fighter and W.H. Tildesley Ltd of Clifford Works, Willenhall currently produce forgings for Harrier fighters. To try and list them all would be an impossible task ranging as they do from the nuts and bolts provided by G.K.N. and Rubery-Owen, but a listing of many of them appears in Appendix 6.

APPENDIX I

Aircraft Built in the Black Country

Star Engineering Co., Frederick Street, Wolverhampton

1910	Star monoplane (40 h.p. Star)	
1911	Star monoplane (50 h.p. Star)	Rebuilt 1910 monoplane; one flight only
1910	Star biplane	Pusher biplane, forward elevator

J. Hartill, Cleveland Street, Wolverhampton

1910	Hartill monoplane (20 h.p. Alveston)	Short hops only

Seddon/Accles & Pollock, Oldbury

1910	Seddon *Mayfly* (2 No. New Engine 65 h.p.)	Never flew

J.S. Foley, Stourbridge

1910	Foley biplane (an all-English engine)

Walter Davies, Dudley

1911	Davies No. 1 biplane glider
1913	Davies No. 2 biplane glider

Sunbeam Car Co., Upper Villiers Street, Wolverhampton

1914	Short 827 Seaplane (Sunbeam Mohawk)	Serials 3093–3112 8630–8649
1915	Short Bomber (Sunbeam Mohawk)	Serials 9356–9370
1915	Short 320 Seaplane (Sunbeam Cossack)	Serials N1360–N1389 N1690– N1709
1916	Avro 504B Trainer (Gnome, Avro 504B/J Trainer Le Rhone, Avro 504J and Dyak) Avro 504K	Serials N5250–N5279 N6130–N6159 D4361–4560 F2533–F2632 H1896–H2076
1917	Sunbeam Bomber (Sunbeam Arab) (Sunbeam No. 171)	Serial N515 N516 ordered, no record of completion

Birmingham & Midland Carriage Company, Middlemore Lane, Smethwick

1918	Handley-Page 0/400	Serials D5401–D5450
		F301–F320
		J2242–J2275
		Cancelled (J2276–J2291)
1918	de Havilland DH 10	Serials E6037–E6136

R. & D. Weaver, Wolverhampton

G-AEME	Henri Mignet HM.14 Flying Flea c/n W.B.1.	Homebuilt 26.8.36. Registration cancelled Dec. 1937

Boulton Paul Aircraft Ltd, Pendeford Lane

Hawker	K5683–K5741	First one flew 21.8.36
Demon	K5898–K5907	
	K8181–K8217	Last flown December 1937
Blackburn Roc	L3057–L3192	L3057 First flew 23.12.38; crashed 3.12.39; production ended August 1940
Defiant	K8310	First prototype, first flight 11.8.37
	K8620	Second prototype, first flight 18.5.39
Defiant I	L6950 L6951–L7036	Initial order of 87; first aircraft flown 30.7.39; tested with bomb racks August 1939
	N1535–N1582 N1610–N1653 N1671–N1706 N1725–N1773 N1788–N1812	Batch of 202 ordered February 1938; N1550 and N1551 fitted with Merlin XX in 1940 as prototype Mk. IIs; N1671 preserved RAF Museum; N1766 parts recovered from crash site
	N3306–N3405 N3421–N3460 N3477–N3520	Batch of 161 ordered May 1938
	T3911–T3960 T3980–T4010 T4030–T4076 T4100–T4141	Batch of 150 ordered December 1939

	V1106–V1141	Batch of 50 ordered
	V1170–V1183	February 1940
	AA281–AA330	Batch of 270 ordered July 1940
	AA350–AA362	
	AA363–AA369	Converted to Defiant 2 in production
Defiant 2	AA370–AA384	Order changed to Defiant 2 standard
	AA398–AA447	
	AA469–AA513	
	AA531–AA550	
	AA566–AA595	
	AA614–AA633	Converted to T.T.Mk.1s before use
	AA651–AA670	Converted to T.T.Mk.1s before use; delivery complete January 1942
Defiant	DR863–DR896	Batch of 140 target tugs
TT.Mk.1	DR914–DR949	ordered July 1942;
	DR961–DR991	prototype delivered
	DS121–DS159	31 January 1942
Fairey		
Barracuda II	DP855–DP902	Order of 300, first flying
	DP917–DP955	August 1943; DP855
	DP967–DP999	converted to Mk.III
	DR113–DR162	prototype; DP872 recovered
	DR179–DR224	from Irish bog. To be restored
	DR291–DR335	DR237–DR275 for Fleet Air Arm Museum
Barracuda III	MD811–MD859	Order of 600, only 392
	MD876–MD924	delivered.
	MD945–MD992	MD963 centre section
	ME104–ME152	from crash site under
	ME166–ME210	restoration in Derby
	ME223–ME270	(crashed 29.7.45)
	ME282–ME293	
	RJ759–RJ799	
	RJ902–RJ948	
	RJ963–RJ966	
(208 No.	Serials RJ967–999, and RK111–323 cancelled.)	

Hawker Fury
     X   VB857   Sea Fury prototype. Final
                                         assembly by Hawker
                                         Aircraft

Balliol
    T.Mk.1   VL892   First flight with Bristol
                                         Mercury engine 30.5.47.
                                         Later re-engined
               VL917   First single-engined turbo-
                                         prop aircraft in the world
                                         24.3.48 (A.S. Mamba
                                         engine)
               VL925   Third prototype
               (VL935   Fourth prototype not built)
Balliol
    T.Mk.2   VW897–VW900   Merlin engined prototypes
                                         first flight 10.7.48
               VR590–VR606   Pre-production batch
               WF989   First of 132 Boulton Paul-built
               WF990–998   production aircraft
               WG110–159   (WG224, 226, 227, and 230
               WG173–187   became CA310, 301, 302,
               WG206–230   and 311 of the Royal
               WN132–171   Ceylon Air Force)

               XF672–673   Replacements for a/c sent to
               XF929–931   Ceylon

Sea Balliol   Prototype converted T.2,
                                         VR599, first flight 10/52

T.21   WL715–WL734
               WP324–WP333   Last delivered 7.12.54
P.111   VT935   Delta wing research a/c. First
                                         flew 6.10.50; converted to
                                         P.111A, 1953
P.112   Mock-up only, two-seat basic
                                         trainer
P.119   Mock-up only, two-seat jet
                                         trainer
P.120   Delta wing research a/c. First
                                         flew 6.8.52; crashed
                                         29.8.52.

Wolverhampton Aviation Ltd, Pendeford Airport

G-ALCS   Miles Gemini 3A c/n WAL/c.1001   Assembled 5.4.50; converted
                                              to Gemini 3C July 1957

G-AMDE   Miles Gemini 3A c/n WAL/c.1002   Assembled 30.3.51; sold to
                                              L.S. Dawson, Yorks Flying
                                              Club

G-AMGF   Miles Gemini 3A c/n WAL/c.1003   Assembled 27.3.51; sold to
                                              Shell Refining & Marketing

G-ALMV   Miles Gemini 3A c/n WAL/c.1004   Assembled 6.10.51; sold to
                                              Fairway Eng., Barton

G-AMKZ   Miles Gemini 3A c/n WAL/c.1005   Assembled 22.12.52; sold to J.
                                              Brockhouse & Co., Wolves.

G-AMME   Miles Gemini 3A c/c WAL/c.1006   Assembled 1.7.52; sold to Ind
                                              Coope & Allsop Ltd,
                                              Wolves.

K. Sedgewick, Grasmere Close

G-AVEY   Super Wot   Version of the Currie Wot
                                              home-built biplane. First
                                              flown 10.1.71

P.G. Bannister, Wolverhampton

G-ARUL   Le Vier Cosmic Wind   Total rebuild of racing aircraft
                                              which crashed Halfpenny
                                              Green 29.8.66. Finished
                                              1972

D. Bateman, Penn

G-A   Taylor J.T.1 monoplane   Home-built monoplane. First
                                              flown 6.6.75 (the last
                                              aircraft built in the Black
                                              Country?)

APPENDIX II

Surviving Aircraft and Aero-Engines Built in the Black Country

Hawker Demon – Aero Vintage Ltd, East Sussex
Serial K8203   25 and 64 Squadron, No. 9 Bombing and Gunnery School, and No. 9 Air Observer School (2292M) – under reconstruction to flying condition

Boulton Paul Defiant I – Royal Air Force Museum, Hendon
Serial N1671   6 M.U. (7.8.40), 307 Sqd. (17.9.40), 6 M.U. (14.1.41), 307 Sqd.(13.3.41), 43 Group D/A (10.6.41), 46 M.U. (8.10.41), 153 Sqd. (30.10.41), 285 Sqd. (22.6.42) Modified to Mark II standards, 10 M.U. (16.5.43), 52 M.U. (8.9.43)
Displayed in 307 Sqd. colours, coded EW–D

Boulton Paul Defiant I – Manchester Museum of Science & Technology
Serial N1766   Engine and propeller only. A 96 Squadron Defiant which crashed in the Peak District in April 1941. Pilot and gunner bailed out. The remains were excavated in 1984

Boulton Paul Defiant I – Moray Firth
Serial L7035   Submerged 50 yards from shore in the Moray Firth where it was ditched 4 May 1942, serving with Two Air Gunners School, Dalcross

Fairey Barracuda II – Fleet Air Arm Museum, Yeovilton (Boulton Paul-built)
Serial DP872   Crash remains salvaged from a Lough Enagh bog, Northern Ireland. Crashed 29.8.44 with 1796 Sqd.

Boulton Paul Balliol T.2 – Katunayake, Sri Lanka
CA310   Preserved at the home of the No. 4 Helicopter Air Wing

Boulton Paul Balliol T.2 – Boulton Paul Society, Wolverhampton
Serial WN149   Rescued from a Salford scrapyard. Under restoration
Serial WN534   Rescued with WN149

Boulton Paul Balliol T.2 – North East Aircraft Museum, Sunderland
Serial WN516   Cockpit section only. Rescued from scrapyard

Boulton & Paul Sea Balliol T.21 – Cosford Aerospace Museum, Wolverhampton
Serial WL732   Ex-Anthorn, Lossiemouth, Boscombe Down

Boulton Paul P.111A – Midland Air Museum, Coventry Airport
Serial VT935   Ex-Cranfield

Boulton Paul P.120 – Midland Air Museum, Coventry
Tailplane only   Test specimen, ex-Hatfield

Currie Super Wot – Dunkeswell, Devon
G-AVEY   Home-built by K. Sedgewick, now privately owned and flown

Surviving Aero-Engines built in Wolverhampton

Star 1911 – Royal Air Force Museum, Hendon
                         1911 Four-cyl. in-line water-cooled 50 h.p.
Sunbeam Gurkha – Fleet Air Arm Museum, Yeovilton
                         (In front fuselage Short 184 (Serial 8359))
                         1915 Side valve V12 11.4 litres 245 h.p.
Sunbeam Nubian II – Science Museum, Kensington
                         1916 Twin OHC V8 7.6 litres 155 h.p.
Sunbeam Dyak – Qantas Airlines, Sydney
                         1917 Straight Six, 110 h.p. Fitted to Avro 504K (ex-A3-4);
                         painted as Qantas' first aircraft
Sunbeam Maori II – Imperial War Museum, Duxford
                         1917 V12, 270 h.p. Serial No. 2/320/116
Sunbeam Maori II – Musée de l'Air, Paris
                         1917 V12, 270 h.p.
Sunbeam Manitou I – IMI-Marston Heritage Centre, Wolverhampton
                         1919 V12 305 h.p., Serial No. 65665. Acceptance test 4 February
                         1919. Never fitted to an aircraft
Sunbeam Manitou version – National Motor Museum, Beaulieu
                         1920 Twin OHC V12 18 litres 350 h.p. fitted to Sunbeam racing
                         car which broke world land speed record
Sunbeam Matabele version – National Motor Museum, Beaulieu
                         1927 Twin OHC V12 18 litres 500 h.p. Two fitted to a Sunbeam
                         200 m.p.h. world land speed record-breaking car
ABC Dragonfly – Science Museum, Kensington
                         1918 nine cyl. radial 300 h.p. nominal (as ordered from Clyno &
                         Guy Motors)

APPENDIX III

Aero-Engines Built in the Black Country

Sunbeam Motors, Wolverhampton

Name	cyl.	litres	h.p.	wt (lb)	Valves	Year	Ordered	Built
unnamed			100	n/a			7	7
Crusader	V8	7.6	145	630	side	1914	224	224
Zulu	V8	9.4	170	640	side	1914	75	75
Mohawk	V12	11.4	215	950	side	1914	287	287
Gurkha	V12	14.0	255	960	side	1915	83	83
Cossack	V12	18.2	310	1372	twin OHC	1916	382	350
Nubian	V8	7.6	155	684	twin OHC	1916	50	36
Afridi	V12	11.4	225	745	twin OHC	1916	300	299
				(100	converted to Maoris)			
Maori I	V12	12.3	250	1065	twin OHC	1917	1063	974
II	V12	12.3	260	1080	twin OHC	1918	(Totals)	
III	V12	12.3	275	1080	twin OHC	1918		
IV	V12	12.3	275	1080	twin OHC	1918	for airships	
Tartar	V12	n/a	300	n/a	n/a	1917	experimental	
Manitou	V12	15.4	325	1050	twin OHC	1917	840	13
Amazon	str.6	9.2	160	747	twin OHC	1916	100	77
Matabele	V12	18.2	400	1000	twin OHC	1916		
Saracen	str.6	9.2	200	740	twin OHC	1916		
Viking	W18	17.4	475	1430	twin OHC	1916	50	9
Dyak	str.6	8.8	110	600	single OHC	1916	160	
Spartan	V12	n/a	200	n/a	n/a	1917	experimental	
Arab	V8	12.3	208	550	single OHC	1917	2110	590
Kaffir	W12		300			1918		
Malay	X20		500			1918		
Bedouin	A8		200			1918	Inverted Arab	
Sikh	V12	64.0	850	1952	push rod	1918		
Semi-Sikh	str.6	32.0	425	1190	push rod	1918		
Pathan	str.6	8.8	100	unknown	diesel	1925		
Sikh III	V12	64.0	1000	1952	push rod	1928		

Licensed-produced Sunbeam engines
Sunbeam Arab

	Ordered	Delivered
Austin Motors	2000	411
Lanchester	600	83
Napiers	450	111
Willys Overland (USA)	1000	116

Sunbeam Cossack

	Ordered	Delivered
Sterling Engines (USA)	n/a	n/a

Guy Motors, Wolverhampton

Type	Configuration	Capacity	h.p.	Ordered	Delivered
ABC.Wasp	seven cyl. radial	11 litres	170	12	1
ABC Dragonfly	nine cyl. radial	23 litres	305	600	1
Guy	V12	under development			

Clyno Engineering, Wolverhampton

ABC Dragonfly	nine cyl. radial	23 litres	305	500	4

Star Engineering, Wolverhampton

Type	Configuration		h.p.	Ordered	Delivered
Star (1910)	four cyl. in-line		40		1
Star (1911)	four cyl. in-line		50		1
Renault (1918)	V8		80	400	12

APPENDIX IV

Aircraft Operated by Don Everall (Aviation) Ltd

de Havilland Dragon Rapide	– G-AGDP, 'GLR, 'KZO,
Auster Autocrat	– G-AHAP, 'IJZ, 'JVV
Auster Alpha	– G–AHST, 'IBZ
de Havilland Tiger Moth	– G-ANJK, 'NME
Douglas DC-3	– G-AMSF, 'NEG
Vickers Viking	– G-AKBG, 'MNL
Piper PA-22 Colt	– G-ARKP, 'RNI, 'RON
Piper 150 Caribbean	– G-ARIL
Piper PA-28 Cherokee 160	– G-ARVR
Cessna 172F	– G-ATBT
Beagle Terrier	– G-ASYG, 'SZE

Further Pendeford residents

Miles Messenger 2A	G-AHUI	–	E.C. Francis
	G-AHZU	–	Tractor Spares Ltd
	G-AJOC	–	C.E. Hickman
	G-AJKK	–	Ductile Steels Ltd
	G-AILL	–	Air Schools Ltd
	G-AJOE	–	Reproducers & Amplifiers Ltd
	G-AKDF	–	L.M. Ferrer
	G-AKKM	–	G.V. Barnett
	G-AKIM	–	Wolverhampton Aero Club
Miles Messenger 4A	G-AJDF	–	B. Williams
	G-ALAH	–	E.P. Jenks
	G-ALAI	–	L.W. Hamp
	G-ALAJ	–	L.M. Ferrer
Miles M.28 Mercury	G-AHAA	–	K.E. Millard & Co.
Miles Hawk Trainer	G-AHNV	–	Wolverhampton Aero Club
	G-AMBN	–	Wolverhampton Aero Club

Miles Hawk Speed 6	G-AGDP	–	R.R. Paine
Miles Gemini	G-AKGE	–	Goodyear Tyre & Rubber Co.
Miles Aerovan	G-AJOF	–	Wolverhampton Aviation
Airspeed Oxford	G-AHTW	–	Boulton Paul Aircraft Ltd
Percival Q.6	G-AHOM	–	Ductile Steels Ltd
de Havilland Rapide	G-AKPA	–	Midland Metal Spinning Ltd
Beech Queen Air	G-ASIU	–	Sir Alfred McAlpine & Son Ltd
Tipsy Nipper	G-APYB	–	P.G. Bannister
Kensinger KF	G-ASSV	–	P.G. Bannister
Le Vier Cosmic Wind	G-ARUL	–	P.G. Bannister
Percival Proctor	G-AHTE		
Druine D.5 Turbi	G-APFA	–	K. Sedgewick
Chrislea CH.3 Super Ace	G-AKVF	–	D.L. Rugg-Easey
Auster J.5L	G-APVG	–	D. Wilson
Piper Tri-Pacer	G-ARIB	–	P. Bannister and J. Marsh

APPENDIX V

Barnstormers and Air Circus Aircraft

Berkshire Aviation Tours Ltd

G-EAKX	– Avro 504K	two-seat trainer
G-EBKB	– Avro 504K	
G-EBKR	– Avro 504K	
G-EBKX	– Avro 504K	

Cornwall Aviation Company

G-EBIZ	– Avro 504K	
G-EBNR	– Avro 504K	
G-EBSE	– Avro 504K	
G-AAAF	– Avro 504K	
G-AAYI	– Avro 504K	
G-ABHI	– Avro 504K	
G-AAUJ	– Avro 504K	
G-ACAF	– Simmonds Spartan	three-seat trainer

Sir Alan Cobham's Air Circus

G-ABSI	– Airspeed Ferry *Youth of Britain II*	ten-seater
G-ABSJ	– Airspeed Ferry	
G-EBYW	– Avro 504K	two-seat trainer
G-ABVH	– Avro 504N	
G-ACCX	– Avro 504N	
G-ACOD	– Avro 504N	
G-ACRS	– Avro 504N	
G-ACOK	– Avro 504N	
G-ACLU	– Avro 504 Genet Major	two-seat trainer
G-ACOZ	– Avro 504	
G-ACPB	– Avro 504	
	BAC.VII	two-seat glider
G-AALH	– Blackburn Lincock	single-seat fighter
G-ABFZ	– Cierva C.19 Mk.IVP	autogyro

G-ABGB – Cierva C.19
G-ACYH – Cierva C.19
G-ABUG – Cierva C.19 Mk.IVP   autogyro
               Comper Swift   single-seat monoplane
G-ACEY – de Havilland Fox Moth   four-seat airliner
G-ACEZ – de Havilland Tiger Moth
G-ABUL – de Havilland Tiger Moth   trainer
               Desoutter I   three-seat cabin monoplane
G-ABYX – Handley Page Clive   22-seat airliner
               Handley Page W.10   eighteen-seat airliner
               Rhon Buzzard   single-seat glider
G-ABBN – Southern Martlet   single-seat biplane
G-ADFZ – Westland Wessex
               Henri Mignet HM.14 Pou-de-Ciel

NB All aircraft used were not owned by Cobham; various other companies provided aircraft such as Air Travel Ltd, and the Cornwall Aviation Co. Different aircraft were used at different times, there usually being fifteen to twenty on a tour. The aircraft used on the winter tours of South Africa were completely different.

British Hospitals Air Pageant

               – BAC Drone single-seat powered glider
               – de Havilland Dragon eight-seat airliner
               – de Havilland Fox Moth (John Pugh)
               – de Havilland Gipsy Moth (Charles Scott)
               – de Havilland Tiger Moth
               – Fairey Fox single-engined bomber
G-ABVG – Parnall Miles-Stayr (Mrs Victor Bruce) one-seat biplane
               – Simmonds Spartan (Pauline Gower) three-seat biplane

NB The Cornwall Aviation Co. also supplied Avro 504Ks and its Simmonds Spartan.

APPENDIX VI

Some Black Country Ancillary Component Manufacturers

Accles & Pollock, Oldbury – metal tubing
Aston-Stedall Aluminium Warehouses Ltd, Tipton
Birmingham Aluminium Casting (1903) Co., Smethwick
Britool Ltd, Wolverhampton
J. Brockhouse & Co. Ltd, Wednesbury
Clifford Products Ltd, Wednesbury – fabrications
Dowty Boulton Paul Ltd, Wolverhampton
Dudley Drop Forging Co. Ltd, Dudley – forgings
Equator Wheels & Sections Ltd, Wolverhampton – rollings, formings
Fafnir Bearing Co. Ltd, Wolverhampton
Ferro Enamels Ltd, Wombourne – coatings
Fischer Bearings Ltd, Wolverhampton – ball and roller bearings
GKN Screws & Fasteners Ltd, Smethwick – nuts, bolts, fasteners
Goodyear Tyre & Rubber Co. Ltd, Wolverhampton – wheels, tyres, brakes
H.M. Hobson Ltd, Wolverhampton
Hampson Industries Ltd, West Bromwich
Helliwells Ltd, Walsall – major components and servicing
N. Hingley & Sons (Netherton) Ltd, Netherton, Dudley
Industrial Furnaces Ltd, Brierley Hill
Intergral Ltd, Wolverhampton – hydraulic and electrical pumps
J.H. Lavender & Co. Ltd, West Bromwich – aluminium castings
Light-Metal Forgings Ltd, Oldbury – forgings
John Marston Ltd, Wolverhampton – aircraft radiators
Excelsior Ltd, Wolverhampton
Marston-Palmer Ltd, Wolverhampton – heat exchangars, fuel tanks
Midland Aeroequipment Ltd, Bloxwich – locks and fastenings
William Mills Ltd, Wednesbury – castings
L.B. Parkes & Co. Ltd, Walsall – pressings, stampings, tanks
Portway Forgings Ltd, Wednesbury – forgings
Reaves Industrial Furnaces Ltd, Wednesbury
Charles Richards & Sons Ltd, Darlaston – nuts and bolts
Rubery, Owen & Co. Ltd, Wednesbury, nuts, bolts, components
George Salter & Co. Ltd, West Bromwich – springs and bearings

Simon Engineering Dudley Ltd, Dudley
Herman Smith Ltd, Dudley
Smethwick Drop Forgings, Smethwick – forgings
Steel Equipment Co. Ltd, West Bromwich
Thompson Bros. (Bilston) Ltd, Bilston – undercarriages etc. (WWI)
Viltool Ltd, Willenhall

APPENDIX VII

National Aviation Days: West Midlands Dates

1932

27	April	–	Kidderminster
28	April	–	Worcester
9	May	–	Walsall
28	May	–	Birmingham
29	May	–	Birmingham
9	June	–	Stoke
13	June	–	Stafford
13	July	–	Kettering
31	August	–	Shrewsbury
9	October	–	Birmingham

1933

No. 1 Tour

5	May	–	Evesham
6	May	–	Birmingham
7	May	–	Birmingham
10	May	–	Kidderminster
11	May	–	Burton-on-Trent
2	June	–	Lichfield
15	June	–	Oswestry
27	July	–	Stoke
29	July	–	Redditch
30	July	–	Wolverhampton
31	July	–	Nuneaton
3	August	–	Burton-on-Trent
5	October	–	Worcester

No. 2 Tour

1	June	–	Walsall
2	June	–	Leominster
6	June	–	Stone
7	June	–	Malvern
8	June	–	Shrewsbury
9	June	–	Bridgnorth
10	June	–	Solihull
11	June	–	Solihull
12	June	–	Tamworth
27	June	–	Leek

1934

22	April	– Birmingham
23	April	– Leek
7	June	– Stoke
8	June	– Walsall
9	June	– Birmingham
10	June	– Birmingham
17	June	– Birmingham
19	June	– Worcester
20	June	– Kidderminster
15	July	– Wolverhampton
19	Sept.	– Burton-on-Trent
21	Sept.	– Kettering

1935

18	April	– Malvern
19	April	– Birmingham
20	April	– Birmingham
21	April	– Dudley
22	April	– Dudley
6	June	– Wolverhampton
9	June	– Birmingham
10	June	– Birmingham

The Astra Tour

6	Sept.	– Cosford
16	Sept.	– Nuneaton
18	Sept.	– Kidderminster
19	Sept.	– Burton-on-Trent
20	Sept.	– Walsall
22	Sept.	– Wolverhampton

The Ferry Tour

8	Sept.	– Cannock

APPENDIX VIII

The Boulton Paul Society

In 1991 Dowty Boulton Paul Ltd began trading as Dowty Aerospace, and the name Boulton Paul disappeared from in front of the factory, apart from a small brass plate. Alarmed that the name of another aircraft manufacturer was disappearing, a group of mostly ex-employees formed the Boulton Paul Society, with the simple aim of preserving the history of the company.

Their first project towards this aim was to create an extensive exhibition of the company's history. Both Dowty Aerospace, and its former parent, Boulton & Paul Ltd, of Norwich, provided sponsorship towards this project, and the exhibition opened at the Aerospace Museum, Cosford, in March 1993. Further locations for the exhibition are envisaged, and new and different exhibits will be arranged at each new site.

In May 1993 the Society obtained the cockpit sections of two Balliols, WN149, and WN534, which had been rescued from a scrapyard by the Pennine Aviation Museum, and transported them back to the factory where they were made. In a workshop made available by Dowty Aerospace these will be restored to exhibition standard, one as an RAF T.2, and the other as a Mamba-engined T.1. A target date of March 1997 has been set for the completion of one, the fiftieth anniversary of the Balliol's first flight.

Also in May 1993 the Boulton Paul Society took over the administration of the Dowty Boulton Paul Archives. They began the huge task of cataloguing them, and handle all queries relating to the company's history.

Although mainly concerned with Boulton Paul, the Society is interested in all aspects of the region's aeronautical activities, and welcomes all like-minded individuals, who are anxious to help preserve the fact that there really used to be aviation in the Black Country.

Anxious to preserve the initials BPA, the Society has decided, as from 1 January 1994, to change its name to the Boulton Paul Association.

INDEX